The Bettin as a Guide t

CW00590420

Malcolm Howard

Raceform Limited
Compton, Newbury. Berkshire, RG20 6NL
01635 578080

Printed and bound in Great Britain
by Greenshires Limited.,

ISBN 1-901100-96-0

Introduction

My first five books for Raceform were all about one concept - value. The logic behind this concept was that bookmakers win because the odds they devise give a margin in their favour and therefore punters only have a chance if their ability to select winners compared to random (the pin method) exceeded this advantage. In other words, if bookmakers bet to margins of 125.0%, giving them a gross margin of 20 per cent, punters could only win in the long term if their selections bettered random by more than this 20 per cent.

Careful study of form and specialist publications such as *Raceform,* together with their expertise in producing ratings for each horse running, would enable punters to have an advantage over random selection and ordinary punters not so well informed. But clearly there would be a limit as to how much advantage could be achieved and accordingly it had to hold true that betting should be restricted to those races where bookmakers were betting to lower than average margins.

Critics of this concept suggested that it had the flaw that it ignored market forces. There would be times that a particular horse would not have 'value' odds only because its connections had fancied and backed it, and worse, another horse might appear to have value odds only because its connections knew it could not win. These critics argued that the betting market was similar to financial markets, which ran contrary to the standard economic relationship between price and demand. In such markets, increasing prices may induce purchasing while reducing prices could have the opposite effect. Investors will buy a share when the price is rising, in the hope that it will rise further and may sell a share when the price is falling if they are concerned that the price may fall further. For the same reason, falling prices may persuade a punter to back a horse as he believes that such reductions reflect inside information, while increasing prices indicate that there is no confidence in the horse.

The main difficulty in following the market this way, without further research, is that we do not know whether changes in the price of a particular horse reflect insider trading (betting by those connected to a particular horse, having superior knowledge than those relying on information available to the general public) or bookmakers merely trying to stimulate business. For example, a particular horse might open at 4/1 and then drift out to 8/1 as there is no interest. Bookmakers, wishing to balance their books. might then reduce the odds to (say) 13/2 to create the illusion that the horse has been backed.

Academic literature appearing in economic journals suggested that the correlation between the number of runners and the sum of the prices (the betting margin in the bookmakers' favour) was due largely to insider trading. This assertion is potentially alarming as the betting margin in most races appears to correlate with the number of runners. Worse, as we approach the new millennium, it was reported that several jockeys had been arrested, but released on bail, for alleged race fixing, and one well known bookmaker was reported to be contemplating retirement on the grounds that the game was 'not as straight as it used to be'.

These concerns prompted the question as to whether the concept of value was still valid or whether it lay strangled under a compost of corruption. The only way to find out was to research the betting market. The main conclusion is that within the limitation that no industry can be totally free of those who wish to sail close to the line, the evidence suggests that the Jockey Club is doing a good job is ensuring that the industry is run as honestly as possible.

In about eighty per cent of all races, there is not (if at all) sufficient insider trading to have an impact on the market and in such cases the concept of value still holds true, but there is evidence that in the remaining twenty per cent of all races the market may be impacted by those having superior knowledge. In a small proportion, about one and a half per cent of all races, such insider trading relates to horses, mostly with unexposed form, not considered to have a realistic chance by the market. These horses can be identified before the race is run in which they are likely to win, thereby, occasionally, giving punters an exciting betting possibility. Readers are invited to read on to work out how to find these potential winners.

CONTENTS

List of Tables

List of Figures

Chapter 1
An overview of the racing and betting industries

1.1 The racing industry

The betting market is often compared with financial markets, but there is one significant difference between the two. Those investing in financial markets expect to make a profit, while those involved in the racing industry, apart from trainers, jockeys and bookmakers, do not.

The owners of companies, the shareholders, expect those employed to run the company, the Board of Directors and their staff, to make a profit. Shareholders expect to share in this profit, through dividends. The prime measurement of success is an increasing share price, which comes about through growth, by achieving competitive advantage. The company has developed a strategy to establish which products are required by the market and the right quality and price associated with those products enabling it to beat the competition.

On the other hand, owners in the racing industry might wish to see their assets (racehorses) grow in value, but this is more in hope than expectation. The Home Affairs Committee of the House of Commons in summing up the evidence put to it wrote:

"Furthermore, the industry is not simply driven by profit. It has the characteristics of a hobby as well as an industry. Owners are prepared to put money in without expecting the return they would expect from conventional investments. The Duke of Devonshire recently told the House of Lords that owning racehorses was like sailing or shooting. One did not expect to make money out of it. Lord Zetland thought this view was out of date, but the Bookmakers' Committee believed that racing was a 'prestigious hobby, not necessarily a commercial enterprise", while the Racegoers Club pointed out that 'no-one .... is forced into racehorse ownership." As the TGWU told us 'owners do not come into it for the purpose of winning money, they come into it to win prestige' " (Home Affairs Committee 1990/91 (a) p xi)

Investors expect a positive return when they buy shares. They accept they are taking a (relatively small) risk when they buy shares in quoted companies and do so because they hope the returns they get will be higher than the risk free rate. To help them make decisions, they can seek informed opinion from stockbrokers or, if they are skilled, form a judgement from public information such as published accounts. In addition, certain share tipping services are available. Risk can be reduced through diversification and it has been shown that risk decreases as diversification increases. If it were possible to buy all shares in a particular market, in proportion to each company's relative size in that market, then its mean positive return could be expected.

Those investing in the racing industry, whether owners or punters, have a negative expected value. Like owners, punters hope to make profits, but, again like owners, only those lucky enough to be at the top of the pile will do so. To help punters make decisions, they can utilise specialist public information such as the official Form Book, as published by *Raceform*, or they can study professional ratings as shown, for example, in *Raceform on Saturday*. As with shares, there are tipping services available, but unlike share tipping which is subject to the Financial Services Act, there is no corresponding regulation overseeing racing tips.

Directors of companies are expected to have skills in human relations, marketing, strategy, knowledge of their particular industry and finance. Trainers must maintain similarly high standards. Their specialist skill starts with the ability to look at an ungainly yearling, yet recognise latent talent. Marketing skills include managing to persuade a potential owner that his training skills will turn the leggy baby he sees into a classic racehorse. Human relations' skills are probably the most important facet for a trainer as the baby takes longer to mature than expected, suffers one setback after another, fails to appreciate that a starting stall opening is the cue to run and just does not appreciate that the idea is to get back to the stables faster than anyone else. Strategy and finance skills come together in trying to find a race so awful that the baby will forget his antipathy towards turf and right handed tracks and will appreciate that the expensive very light shoes he is wearing are there for a reason.

Another major difference between the financial sector and the racing industry is 'insider trading' This is defined as trading by individuals, such as directors of a company, or the owners of a racehorse, who have superior knowledge compared to the general public. With regard to the financial sector, insider trading, if allowed, could give those in the know a guaranteed and an unfair advantage. For example, if a share was quoted at £2.30 and the directors had at hand a takeover bid at £3.40 per share, then they could buy at the market price with almost impunity. Of course, financial regulators try to ensure such dealing cannot happen and all company directors are under an obligation to report to the City any significant information, as it happens. 'Significant information' would include such things as a takeover bid and where the directors knew that financial results about to be announced would cause a movement in the share price as they were meaningfully different than market expectations.

Insider trading in the racing industry can have no such guarantees. The owner and trainer might have superior knowledge about a particular horse, but it is very unlikely that they would have a detailed knowledge of every racehorse running in the race their horse was entered for. For this reason, insider trading in the racing industry is not illegal, although jockeys are not allowed to bet on the grounds that they can exert influence over a race.

Some of the differences between financial and betting markets are shown in Table 1-1.

1.2 The betting industry and the administration of racing

Up until the 1950's, betting on horseracing was only legal if bets were taken on a racecourse or where off-course punters held a credit account, the latter being protected by legislation that a gambling debt was not enforceable in law. Of course, off-course cash betting took place and indeed was thriving. A network of illegal betting shops was connected to factories and other workplace through 'bookies' runners' who collected the bets and returned with the winnings the following day, where applicable. Punters took the risk of not being paid out, but welshing was rare and betting duty was not even at the embryonic stage.

In 1959, the Government concluded that increasing illegal betting was a social evil and the Home Affairs Committee of the House of Commons reported that *"in November 1959 the then Home Secretary appointed a Departmental Committee under the Chairmanship of Sir Leslie Peppiatt, to 'consider whether it is desirable and practicable that persons engaged in betting transactions on horseraces, other than by means of the totalisator, should be required to make a contribution for purposes conducive to the improvement of breeds of horses or the sport of horseracing; and if so, to advise on its amount and the means of securing it'"* (Home Affairs Committee 1990/91, p 18).

The solution to stop illegal gambling was to make it legal, but the concern was that this would cause racecourse attendance to drop and in April 1960 the Peppiatt Committee reported that:

"There is almost unanimous opinion on all sides of the racing industry (including the bookmakers) that a levy is required" ; concluded that *"weighing the evidence as a whole, we consider that a levy is desirable"* ; and recommended a *"levy of £1 million to £1.25 million in the first year of operation"* (£100,000 for breeding and veterinary science; some £250,000 for increased prize money; and some £500,000 - £750,000 for the improvement of amenities on racecourses) (Home Affairs Committee 1990/91, p 18)

The Betting Levy Act 1961 established the Horserace Betting Levy Board (the Levy Board) and following the Betting and Gaming Act 1960, punters found themselves in what has been described as the 'golden age of betting'. For the first time, betting shops were legalised, thereby eliminating the need for ridiculous punters' pseudonyms, adding to enjoyment and security. Bettors could now listen to a race being run live, through the 'blower', without being concerned about a police raid and could be even more confident about being paid out should a winner be selected. Better still, betting shop owners were beginning to improve the level of comfort in their shops and racecourse' amenities were improving to the benefit of racegoers, all at the expense of bookmakers who were contributing almost an equal amount to that of the Tote.

The problem with paradise is that it ends abruptly and so the golden age of betting was shattered by the Betting, Gaming and Lotteries Act 1963, which led to betting duty being totally paid by punters. When betting duty was first introduced it was paid by bookmakers out of their profits. Initially, they asked punters to make only a nominal contribution through the elimination of 'bits' (100/6 became 16/1, 100/7 became 14/1, 100/8 became 12/1 and 100/9 became 11/1) and a reduction in place percentages (one-quarter of the odds for the first three with eight runners or

Table 1-1   The Company and Betting/Racing Environments

	The Company Environment (public companies)	The Racing Environmemt (horse racing)
Owners	Shareholders	Individuals, partnerships and syndicates
The management team	The Board of Directors	The trainer and his team
The market	Various	Racecourses
Market research	Establishing the type of products potential customers will want to buy, together with knowledge of the desired quality and price	Establishing the exact conditions preferred by own and competitors' horses
The product	Various	Training horses to run fast
The competition	Various	Other trainers and their teams
Strategy	To gain competitive advantage and grow the company	To place horses to best advantage
Public information	Published Accounts	The Form Book, prepared by Raceform Limited
Private information	Management Accounts	Private gallops
Betting medium	Making investments	Betting with bookmakers or with the Tote
Intermediaries	Stockbrokers	Bookmakers and the Tote
The betting market	Various stock exchanges	Major off-course bookmakers and racecourse bookmakers
Tipping services	Newspaper tips, and advertised services ranging from good to of doubtful benefit	Newspaper tips, and advertised services ranging from professional down to confidence tricksters
Insider trading	Illegal, but it is difficult to prove	Not illegal, provided the rules of racing have not been broken. Mere betting by owners difficult to prove.
Advised betting strategy	Trying to ensure shares are bought at the right price and decisions are based on proper research, rather than hunch	Trying to ensure that horses are backed at a price that is fair, given the overall probabilities. In other words, 'getting value'.
Key to 'betting' success (for a punter)	Timing of making investments	Knowing when individual horses are going to win
Relatively certain way of being successful at betting	Being a stockbroker	Being a bookmaker
Key factor in decision making	Understanding the market and market movements	Understanding the market and market movements

more, became one-fifth the odds a place, and where one-third of the odds applied, this became one-quarter).

Within a short time, bookmakers had resolved to collect both betting duty and betting levy from the punter, but the concession originally given by punters as their share of duty and levy was never revoked. Within a short time many small independent bookmakers were being bought up by the betting chains, often at what appeared to be inflated prices, and punters were left wondering what was going on. What *was* going on was that the majors had come up with a wheeze to vastly increase profitability and this was charging punters under the guise of 'betting tax' an amount that exceeded their liabilities for duty and betting levy.

Lord Rothschild had chaired a Royal Commission into gambling in 1978 and in their submission into the Home Affairs Committee the Home office stated:

"In the Royal Commission's words 'Provided that punters are not misled, they and the bookmakers should be free to make whatever arrangements they please' It may further be worth noting that the Licensed Betting Office Regulations 1986 require bookmakers to display a notice setting out the terms on which the licensee invites people to bet, including the amount of various deductions from winning bets, any maximum limit on winnings and the procedure for resolving disputes" (Home Affairs Committee 1990/91, p 6)

Bookmakers had argued that they had to pay 'tax on tax' and that as punters could choose whether or not to pay tax on a bet, the total amount collected from punters was always less that their liabilities. The Home Office obviously supported their view as their submission included these words:

" 'Deductions' are a percentage addition to the punter's stake, or a percentage deduction from the punter's winnings if any. The common rate of 'deduction' in either case is, at present, 10 per cent. This is generally said by bookmakers to cover: liability to general betting duty (which is currently 8 per cent of all off-course turnover); the liability to pay levy on turnover on bets on racehorses (likely to equate to some 0.9 per cent on average under the current scheme); and certain non-recoverable VAT payments. Because duty and levy are charges on turnover, bookmakers' liability to them is likely to be greater than simply 8.9 per cent (i.e., the duty plus levy calculated as a percentage). For example, where the punter elects to pay the 'deduction' with the stake, duty and levy are payable on the 'deduction' as well as the stake itself. **Or, where no 'deduction' is paid with the stake and there are no winnings as a result of the bet, duty and levy are payable on the stake, without a deduction having been made in relation to it**" (Home Affairs Committee 1990/91, p 6) **(Author's bold)**

The argument went that when punters did not pay 'tax on' the bookmakers had to pick up all the liabilities. This single argument really was very clever because its acceptance meant that over the years bookmakers' profits were vastly higher than they might have been. The reality, of course, was that punters who did not declare that they were paying any tax were, in fact, paying more tax than their counterparts paying tax on. The reason for this was that as ten per cent was going to be deducted from any winnings, the bookmaker only had a liability against part of the stake. The proof of this is that a £10 bet, tax not paid on, is the same as writing £9 stake plus £1 tax paid, where the tax rate is ten per cent.. The return on this bet will always be the same as £9 stake plus tax 90p = £9.90

The Horserace Levy Board, maybe with more up to date information suggested that:

"Although duty and Levy payments comprise, on average, 8.7 per cent of total turnover, most bets are placed with the deduction expressed as a rate over the pound. Since an 8.7 per cent deduction within the pound is equivalent to a 9.5 per cent deduction over the pound, this is rounded up to give the current deduction of 10 per cent. Bookmakers regard the addition of 0.5 per cent as partly covering the cost of VAT" (Home Affairs Committee 1990/91, p 50)

At the time (1991) it was believed that about 80 per cent of punters did not pay 'tax' on (for example, those punters betting on a straight forecast could not pay tax on, as the tax deduction was built into the computer formula) and the remaining 20 per cent of punters did. Assuming this ratio and assuming bookmakers' liabilities were as projected by the Horserace Levy Board, then bookmakers would (effectively) deduct from punters £98 for every £1,000 of turnover (stake £902 plus £98 tax paid) as against the £87 per £1,000 they paid over. In other words, the benefit of deducting more from punters that they needed to meet their liabilities was more than double that calculated by the Horserace Levy Board. Never can so much profit had been made merely on the basis of how punters wrote out their betting slips and its corresponding interpretation.

The same applies to all rates of betting tax. In 1999, the rate of deduction is generally nine per cent, so a punter who would have a £100 tax free bet on the racecourse, when in a betting shop should proceed as follows:
(1) Multiply £100 by 0.09 (for 9 per cent) = £9.
(2) Deduct this £9 from £100 to arrive at a stake of £91.
(3) Write the bet as £91 stake plus £8.19 deduction = £99.19 staked.

This stake plus deduction of £99.19 will always pay the same as £100 staked, tax not paid on. Note that the savings achieved are lower at a deduction of 9 per cent that they were for ten per cent, so the saving by paying tax on increases the higher the duty rate becomes.

By 1991, the process of buying up the small independent off-course bookmaker had continued at an unrelenting pace and by then three firms had between them an estimated 75 to 80 per cent of the market. BOLA (Betting Offices Licensees Association) reported to the Home Affairs Committee:
"The Home Affairs Committee may also be interested to learn that members of BOLA are esti-mated to be responsible for approaching 90 per cent of the Levy, with three member companies alone contributing an estimated 75-80 per cent" (Home Affairs Committee 1990/91, p 60)

After hearing all the evidence, the Home Affairs Committee were clearly not impressed by the off-course bookmakers in using the words 'betting tax' to refer to betting duty and levy and for using VAT as an excuse for over-deducting from punters. They wrote:
"Despite the evidence of BOLA, Ladbrokes makes no mention of VAT in its 'Fair Play Rules' when the term 'tax' is explained to punters, while the notice displayed in William Hill betting shops refers simply to 'deductions for betting duty and Levy (at 10 per cent).' The notice in Coral shops gives no indication of what deductions are for. **We consider that the use by the bookmak-ers of VAT as a justification for deductions is entirely indefensible."** (Home Affairs Committee 1990/91 (a), p xxviii)

They were also unimpressed about the amount of betting Levy paid by bookmakers and rec-ommended that:
"The Bookmakers' Committee should propose a sum not less than £50 million at today's prices for the 31st Levy. In line with our earlier observations, we do not believe that the modest nature of this increase should need to result in any increase in bookmakers' deductions." (Home Affairs Committee 1990/91 (a), p xxxii)

In its submission to the Home Affairs Committee the Jockey Club/Horse Advisory Council sug-gested that betting levy should be replaced by a royalty system, but this committee believed that racing's administrators would not survive without the security of a statutory framework and inde-pendent arbitration. They wrote:
"From what we have seen, we do not believe that the racing industry at present has the com-mercial skills or unity and clarity of purpose necessary to take on the big bookmakers in the open market. We believe that they would be ill-advised to seek to abandon the current system, and we would be fearful of the consequences for the racing industry of a market free-for-all." (Home Affairs Committee (a), p xxii)

The above paragraph was very important as it led to the formation of the British Horseracing Board (BHB), who were to be responsible for the complete administration of racing, apart from security and discipline, which was to be retained by the Jockey Club.

In addition, several changes came about because of the Home Affairs Committee report. The hours that betting shops could open and the products and services that could be offered in them were extended, Sunday racing was legalised, the fixture list was restructured, taking into account the needs of the horse population, and racecourses were encouraged to maximise their income by attracting new racegoers or diversifying their business.

By the late 1990's, the off-course betting market was still dominated by three major companies and when Ladbrokes bought the Coral chain, they were forced by Ministerial directive to sell the lot, even though they had offered to sell some as a package to ensure they could not dominate any area. The decision to force the sale of the Coral chain of betting offices came about after much pressure from some members of the media, but whether it matters who owns betting shops must be open to question.

In some special races, bookmakers do offer morning prices, but there can be no guarantee that they will be better than 'starting prices', the method upon which most off-course bets are settled. For this reason, all off-course bookmakers are settling most of their bets at the same 'starting price', which in turn can be heavily impacted by one or all of the betting chains.

The Home Affairs Committee expressed the view that all betting shop punters should be made aware that off-course bookmakers hedge bets on-course. They wrote:

"We recommend that new Regulations should be made requiring betting office licensees to publish notices informing customers that deductions are part of the price the bookmaker charges for betting and that deductions are not a tax. Such notices should also indicate that odds in the shop may be affected by hedging bets on-course. Bookmakers may, of course, also wish to display notices about themselves outlining their statutory obligations to pay duty and Levy". (Home Office Affairs Committee (a), p xxix)

Bookmakers argue, with reason, that their hedging activities merely ensure that the final odds (the starting prices) reflect the market as a whole and if they were not allowed this activity the market would become distorted. This market, of course, reflects the cumulative betting from three sources:

Insiders: These are bettors who are connected with a horse racing in a particular race and have superior information. They may be an owner, trainer, stable lad or any person who has close knowledge of the form and fitness of the horse running.

Informed outsiders: These are bettors who have access only to public information, but through studying such public information have better information than 'uninformed outsiders'.

Uninformed outsiders: These are bettors who rely on media' tips, hunch, 'birthdays' and pins and are better suited to gambling medium that are purely random, such as the National Lottery.

Overall, but taking into account the hedging activities of the major off-course bookmakers, there is every reason to believe that the on-course betting market will become more competitive as we approach the new millennium. Traditionally, bookmakers' joints (pitches at the racecourse) were handed down from one generation to another, but over the winter of 1998/9 they are being auctioned off to the highest bidder. New blood entering the ring may lead to competitive prices and smaller betting margins.

1.3 Insider Trading

As discussed earlier, insider trading in the betting industry is not illegal and a distinction must be drawn between this and the rules of racing being broken. Insider trading within racing would only become illegal if it were coupled with trainers not running their horses to the best of their ability. The Jockey Club is responsible for the integrity of racing and while this organisation has often been criticised for its administrative abilities, its honesty, dedication and impartiality have never been questioned.

It must be remembered that the integrity of racing is important to everyone involved in the industry. The Home Affairs Committee reported:

"The Racegoers Club told us that punters 'all have a common interest in the integrity of racing'. This interest should be shared by bookmakers since, as the HBLB told us, 'the integrity of racing........ underpins the whole betting activity. Punters, racegoers, owners and jockeys all want to be assured that the horse which wins a race does so in accordance with the rules of racing and

that no doping or other deceit has been practised. .... This is a service (that part of the Levy paying for security) which is absolutely vital for bookmakers; if racing were corrupt, their market for horseracing bets would collapse" (Home Affairs Committee 1990/91 (a), p xliii)

As shown in Table 2-8 (see chapter 2) the returns from seven racecourses were analyzed over two complete seasons (1997 and 1998). Horses were classified as favourite, second favourite, third favourite, fourth favourite, others with odds up to 14/1 and others 16/1 and upwards Amongst other things, the Tote returns were analysed and this analysis showed that there was no bias between any of the segments. This meant that over a complete season the actual results were consistent with the market, and as there were no market distortions, there is clearly no evidence of any serious problem with regards to the integrity of racing.

Research suggested that some of the races tested had been the subject of insider trading, **but there is no suggestion that the Rules of Racing had been broken nor that the horses, the subject of insider trading, had been prevented from winning any of their races.**

References
Home Affairs Committee (1990/91) **'Levy on Horseracing** - Memoranda of Evidence' *The Home Affairs Committee, Session 1990-91, 16 January 1991,* London: HMSO
Home Affairs Committee (1990/91) (a) **'Levy on Horserace Betting** - Volume I - Fourth Report' *The Home Affairs Committee, Session 1990-91, 17 May 1991,* London: HMSO

Chapter 2
The Betting Market

2.1 Academic literature
Economists have an interest in the betting market as it has many similarities to financial markets, but the former is considered to be much simpler to model, for example, as Shin (1992) states, *"since odds are offered on each horse, all basic securities are traded, thereby ruling out the difficulties associated with incomplete markets."*

Bookmakers act as intermediaries for those who wish to bet in any particular race. Economists believe that those wishing to place a bet fall into two categories, Insiders and Outsiders. Insiders are those connected with a particular horse who will have superior information, while Outsiders must rely on information available to the general public. Outsiders are ordinary punters, who, according to Shin (1992) are *"mechanical traders who do not act strategically, but are payoff maximisers according to their subjective probability judgements."* Shin (1991) described ordinary punters as *" ' noise traders' who cling stubbornly to their beliefs."*

Nevertheless, in the absence of Insiders in the betting market, Shin concedes that ordinary punters (Outsiders) will collectively create such a market. Shin (1992) and/or Shin (1993) states:

"However, although each outsider (taken individually) may be quite irrational, the game (any particular race) is designed so the market prices which follow from outsiders' demands for bets are fully revealing, in the sense that the equilibrium prices coincide with the true probabilities. This provides a benchmark for the general case in which distortions in market prices are introduced as a result of insider trading. When the Insider plays no part in the game the prices will coincide with the true probabilities. In other words, competitive prices are the parimutuel betting odds."

What this suggests is that Tote odds reflect the market, unbiased by insider trading. The logic behind this assertion is that Insiders would generally not bet with the Tote as to do so would be self-defeating, as a sizeable bet would only have the effect of drastically reducing the dividend, should the bet be successful.

Academics believe that Insiders have a significant effect on the betting market operated by bookmakers. Shin (1992) states:

"It would seem, therefore, that the activity of insider traders influences the betting market in a significant way."

Crafts (1985) suggests that there is a sizeable body of evidence, both systematic and anecdotal, which points to the prevalence of insider trading in the market for bets. Such beliefs stem from an admission by the Jockey Club (1968) that:

"Trainers and their staff are insufficiently paid for their services and the majority have to resort to betting to make ends meet."

Economists believe that bookmakers react in several ways to protect themselves from potential losses, suffered as a result of insider trading. According to Shin (1991) the first protection method is to employ the 'square root rule'. He states:

"In particular, it is optimal for the bookmaker to employ a 'square root rule' in which the ratio of posted prices is set equal to the square root of the ratio of winning probabilities. One consequence of this rule is that the betting odds tend to understate the winning chances of the favourites and to overstate the winning chances of the longshots. If the prices were proportional to winning probabilities, the winnings/wager ratio should be consistent over all the subsets. There is a tendency for the bookie to avoid setting very large odds."

What Shin is suggesting is that if the betting market (such as the Tote market) was unaffected by insider trading, then the losses suffered by punters backing favourites would be the same as the losses suffered by punters backing outsiders. The Tote deducts 16 per cent from its win pool, so over the long term, any punter backing with the Tote would expect to recover £84 for every £100 bet. If there were no bias, then punters always backing the favourite would recover £84 for every £100 bet and so would the punter backing all the outsiders, again, in the long term. There would be no bias between favourites and outsiders.

Academics argue that the effect of the bookmakers' square root rule is to ensure that those backing favourites would always do better than those backing outsiders. In the literature this phenomenon became known as the 'favourite/longshot bias'. Many academics have concluded that such 'favourite/longshot bias' exists, but the data set used has been relatively small. Williams and Paton (1997) set out to test whether such bias existed by reviewing all turf races run between 19 March 1992 and 18 May 1992 inclusive. They only included full meetings, with a minimum of six races. In all, they reviewed 5,903 horses running in 510 races. They were interested in comparing the results based on forecast prices with starting prices. Forecast prices were taken from each day's issue of *The Sporting Life* and the starting prices were as declared, being the general price at which a sizeable bet could be placed with bookmakers on the racecourse, immediately prior to the start of the race. Races where not all horses had a forecast price (for example, in a twenty-runner race, sixteen horses may be quoted, but the remaining four would be shown as 33/1 Bar) were eliminated and this left 4,689 horses running in 481 races. There were 45 races with up to five runners, 196 races with between six and ten runners, 144 races with between eleven and fifteen runners, 78 races with between sixteen and twenty runners and 18 races with more than twenty runners. In these races, they found that percentage losses increased as the odds got bigger, thereby supporting the favourite/longshot bias concept. Odds-on backers lost 7.3% of their stakes, but this figure increased to 24.4% for those backing horses at odds against up to 20/1. Intrepid punters backing horses at longer odds than 20/1 lost 64.9% of their stakes. Overall, for every £100 staked, punters retained £70.90.

Shin (1992) concluded from a previous study:

"Thus, our result can be paraphrased as saying that the introduction of the favourite/longshot bias raises the bookies expected profit."

According to Shin (1993) the next method of protection against insider trading used by bookmakers is to increase the margin in their favour. He says:

"Since the bookies must break-even in expected terms, they raise their margins on order to

recoup their loss to the Insider. Given that the spread is increasing with the incidence of insider trading, the size of the observed spread provides some indication of the severity of the market distortion due to insider trading."

The theory is that bookmakers' ability to raise margins to cover for losses suffered by trading with Insiders is limited by the size of the field and that such ability increases as the field size increases, which Shin (1993) suggests, *"lends support to the central prediction of our theoretical model that the sum of the prices is positively correlated with the number of runners."* To emphasise the point he concludes his (1993) paper:

"The key empirical feature at the heart of this paper has been the strong positive correlation between the sum of the prices and the number of runners."

Williams and Paton (1997) challenge Shin's view that the correlation between betting margins and the number of runners is due to insider trading. They suggest that the cause of this correlation is that the punter only counts a fixed fraction of his potential losses and accordingly underestimates the odds against him, or overestimates the chance his selection has of winning. To demonstrate this hypothesis they assume that bettors are risk-neutral and that both bettors and bookmakers have equal access to all publicly available information. In other words, they assume that punters act rationally, with financial acumen, whereas Shin assumes that punters, as individuals, act irrationally.

A key issue, as far as ordinary punters are concerned, is that if insider trading impacts on them because they, in effect, are recovering bookmakers' Insider losses, to what extent is it going on? Shin (1993) suggests:

"The conclusion of our empirical investigation is that the incidence of insider trading in the week of 1 July 1991 was around 2%."

The validity of Shin's statistical calculations was confirmed by Jullien and Salanie (1994) who calculated (based on Shin's data) that the incidence of insider trading was equal to 2.28%, with a standard error of 0.07%.

Williams and Paton (1997) set out to test Shin's conclusions that the incidence of insider trading was around 2%, by analysing their data of 481 races. They separated these races into 62 handicaps of 0-100 or higher and 419 races consisting of non-handicaps and handicaps rated lower than 0-100. Their hypothesis was that these 62 higher grade handicaps would be the subject of particular media attention and accordingly the expectation by bookmakers would be that such races offered very little opportunity for non-disclosure of useful private information. They assumed that the informational content of any private information available about these race types would be close to zero.

They tested both sets of races to assess whether the dependent variable, being the overall betting margin on the race, was affected by various independent variables. These independent variables included the number of runners, the spread of the odds and whether the odds moved down when comparing the forecast odds with the starting prices. The 'spread of the odds' reflected the variation between the shortest price horse in the race (the favourite) and the longest priced outsider. They found that there was a significant correlation between the number of runners and the overall betting margin, but that the correlation weakened where high grade handicaps had lots of runners. In both sets of races, the overall betting margin increased where significant downwards odds movements were detected and decreased as the spread of the odds increased.

Following much statistical analysis on their data set, Williams and Paton decided that their support for the 'fraction' hypothesis was unfounded and they concluded:

"Thus we find that the correlation between the number of runners and the sum of the prices is restricted to races which are not higher grade handicaps. Our results are consistent with Shin's 1993 claim that the link is due largely to insider trading."

The academic literature seems to suggest that favourite/longshot bias is due to bookmakers adopting a 'square root rule', thereby raising their expected profit. Such profit can be worn away by insider dealing, but bookmakers balance their books and recover equilibrium by increasing the betting margins.

The key questions this academic literature raises are:

* Are the assumptions made and statistical analysis valid?

13

Table 2-1 Average betting margins per runner for all races run in Great Britain in June 1996

Grade of race	Number of races	Average betting margin % per runner
A	35	1.68
B	28	1.98
C	70	2.26
D	199	2.36
E	132	2.21
F	104	2.30
G	46	2.32
All races	614	

Example of how to read the margins: A ten runner Grade A race with the average margin of 1.68% per runner would have a betting margin of 16.8%. In the official Form Book, this would be shown as 116.8.

Grade A races' margins were particularly low due to some extremely low values at Epsom and Royal Ascot

Table 2-2 Comparison between the performance of favourites and their expected value (as determined by their starting prices) for all races in Great Britain in June 1996

Grade of race	Number of races	Mean probability of favourites' winning	Expected Value (Number of favs. winning)	Actual number of favourites winning	Bias	% bias as % of Expected Value
A	35	0.640	22	22	0	0.0
B	28	0.553	15	19	4	26.7
C	70	0.624	44	45	1	2.3
D to G	481	0.631	304	332	28	9.2
All races	614	0.628	385	418	33	8.6

Note: The apparent significant bias for grade B races was probably due to a uneven mix of races, which included some very competitive handicaps where the favourites had a mean probability of winning between 0.2 and 0.4 and some non-handicaps for two-year-olds just below top class, with limited form favouring the experienced horses, where the favourites had a mean probability of winning of above 0.6. Two of these major handicaps was won by the clear favourite and one of the first three horses in the betting won five out of the six two-year-old races.

14

* If the academic literature is valid, what impact does it have on the ordinary punter?
* If the academic literature is valid, what can the ordinary punter learn from the market?
The remainder of this chapter sets out to answer these questions.

2.2 Is it just a question of class?

The first question to ask is whether bookmakers' margins increase in line with the number of runners in each race because of insider trading or whether there are other factors affecting this relationship. For example, could it be a matter of class? Class is defined as level of ability and all races are graded according to class. The grades run from A (the highest grade for the best horses) to G (the lowest grade for the worst horses on the Flat).

The top grade is split into several subsections:
Group 1 is the top subsection catering for the very best horses. Races in this category include all the classics (2000 Guineas, 1000 Guineas, Derby, Oaks and St Leger) Coronation Cup, St James's Palace Stakes, Coronation Stakes, Gold Cup (Ascot), Coral-Eclipse Stakes, Juddmonte International Stakes, July Cup, Aston Upthorpe Yorkshire Oaks, King George VI & Queen Elizabeth Diamond Stakes, Nunthorpe Stakes, Sussex Stakes, Haydock Park Sprint Cup, Queen Elizabeth II Stakes, Dubai Champion Stakes and Lockinge Stakes.
Group 2 races are designed for horses just below the very best and include some famous races such as the Dante Stakes, Prince of Wales's Stakes, Jockey Club Stakes, Goodwood Cup, Great Voltigeur Stakes, Falmouth Stakes and Diadem Stakes
Group 3 races and Listed races follow Group 1 and Group 2 races. The vast majority of Grade A races are non-handicaps, but a few high grade handicaps rated 0-105 (such as the Rosemary Rated Stakes Handicap at the Ascot Festival) or better are given Listed status and therefore carry an A grading.
All horses are given a rating (constantly updated) by the British Horseracing Board and any horse can only run in a handicap if that handicap is consistent with a particular horse's rating. For example, a horse rated 100 could not run in a handicap for horses rated 0-80.
Grade B races include the best handicaps and most famous handicaps not given Listed status such as the Lincoln Handicap at Doncaster and Goodwood's Stewards' Cup, which are open to all horses. Most Grade B handicaps are for horses with a rating of 0-105 or 0-110. Grade B races also include non-handicaps designed for horses just below top class.
Grade C races include middle class conditions races and handicaps rated between 0-90 and 0-100.
Grade D races include standard class non-handicaps and handicaps rated between 0-75 and 0-85.
Grades E to G are designed for moderate horses, include claiming and selling races, and handicaps rated between 0-60 and 0-70.

To evaluate whether class had an effect on bookmakers' margins and the favourite/longshot phenomenon, all races run in Great Britain in June 1996 were examined. June was chosen as that month contains a significant number of grade A races due to the Epsom Derby meeting and Royal Ascot. In all, 614 races were inspected.
The first finding (see Table 2-1) was the margins for grade A races was the lowest of all the grades at an average of 1.68 per cent per runner. Margins for grade B races averaged 1.98 per cent per runner, which although higher than for grade A races, was significantly lower than for grade C to grade G races, which varied between 2.21 per cent per runner and 2.36 per cent per runner.
Favourite/longshot bias for each grade was tested by calculating the collective winning probability of the first three in the betting (up to first five in the betting when there were co-favourites) with the remainder of the field in each race. An overall mean probability of the favourites' winning was calculated for each grade and this figure was multiplied by the number of races in each grade to calculate an Expected Value. This Expected Value was the expected number of races which would be won by one of the favourites and was compared to the actual number of races won by one of the favourites, to assess bias (see Table 2-2).

With the exception of grade B races, which was explained by an uneven mix of races in a limited sample, the only significant bias detected was in the lower class races, rated D to G.

Next, the same 614 races were analysed based on the number of runners in each race (see Table 2-3). In this case, bias became significant when the number of runners in a race reached double figures and thereafter there appeared to be a linear relationship. In other words, the bias increased as the number of runners in each race increased. Given these findings, it would appear that if there were a link between betting margins and insider trading, then insider trading primarily took place grade D to G races, where there were ten runners or more in the race. The problem with this analysis, however, is that it is based on the assumption that bookmakers increase margins to equalise the effects of insider trading. A feasible alternative explanation is that the use of a 'square root rule' or some other methods of avoiding laying large odds comes about because of bookmakers' *fear* of insider trading, rather than insider trading itself.

2.3 The betting market re-conceptualised

Box (1976) wrote:

"Since all models are wrong the scientist must be alert to what is importantly wrong. It is inappropriate to be concerned about mice when there are tigers abroad.".

It is important for ordinary punters, with only public information available to them, to have some idea as to the level of inside information effectively being employed against them, as it must follow that bookmakers must at least try to balance their books. Media coverage early in 1999 could have created the impression that the racing industry was falling apart. Several jockeys had been interviewed by the police concerning alleged race fixing, but no charges had been brought. It was reported in *Raceform on Saturday (January 9)* that Stephen Little, a leading bookmaker, was giving up his profession having voiced worries about non-triers, race fixing and possible corruption. Little was quoted as saying:

"It seems that any horse in the betting you can't lay can't win. A few years ago I would often get left with no bets on the favourite or the second favourite, yet a reasonable proportion of them would win. Now they don't seem to win if they are not backed so I just wonder if racing is as straight as it was."

The academic literature suggesting insider trading was based on data earlier than 1997, so as Stephen Little is suggesting deterioration since this period, future prospects for ordinary punters may seem bleak. Set against this, the Jockey Club had in place by the 1990's betting intelligence officers whose job it is to report on irregular betting. Surely, they would spot insider trading if it were at levels that would concern major bookmakers?

In an attempt to ascertain which side is nearer the truth, the starting point will be the hypothesis that favourite/longshot bias is caused by bookmakers' fear of insider trading and that this fear affects the odds in two stages. To illustrate this hypothesis, a theoretical betting market is set up, based on Tote betting (see Table 2-4).

In the theoretical betting market there are eleven horses, which will race against each other in 100 races. The assumed probabilities are that the favourite *(Raceform on Saturday)* will win 25 races in 100, while the rank outsider *(Newspaper Mash)* will win 1 race in 100. At each race, there are one hundred punters, each investing £10 on their chosen selection. It is assumed that Shin's statement *"when the Insider plays no part in the game the prices will coincide with true probabilities and that competitive prices are parimutuel (Tote) betting odds"* (see earlier references) is valid and that accordingly twenty-five punters will back *Raceform on Saturday*, while only one punter will back *Newspaper Mash*.

As there are one hundred punters each staking £10, each Tote pool would amount to £1,000 from which 16 per cent (£160) would be deducted leaving £840 to be distributed amongst the winning ticket holders. If *Raceform on Saturday* won, then there would be 250 winning units (twenty five times £10) giving a dividend of £3.36. If, on the other hand, *Newspaper Mash* won, then there would only be ten winning units and the dividend would be £84. However, provided the results in the long term were consistent with the market (and therefore the pre-calculated probabilities) then all punters would receive 84p for every £1 invested. If each punter invested £10 in one hundred races, giving a total stake of £1,000, then they would each recover £840, over the

Table 2-3 Comparison between the performance of favourites and their expected value (as determined by their starting prices) for all races in Great Britain in June 1996 Analysis by 'number of runners'

Number of runners in each race	Number of races	Mean probability of favourites' winning	Expected Value (Number of favs. winning)	Actual number of favourites winning	Bias	% bias as % of Expected Value
2-3	7	1.000	7	7	0	0.0
4-5	68	0.872	59	61	2	3.4
6-10	316	0.670	212	219	7	3.3
11-15	169	0.514	87	103	16	18.4
16-20	43	0.402	17	21	4	23.5
21 or more	11	0.297	3	7	4	133.3
All races	614	0.628	385	418	33	8.6

Note: The number of runners are presented in bands of five. However, two and three-runner races are separated from four and five-runner races as the former cannot have any bias, given that the first, second or third favourite must win the race.

The mean probability of either the first, second or third favourite winning the race must decline as the number of runners increases, but of course, the Expected Value takes this factor into account. It is noticeable that the bias increases significantly as the number of runners in the race reaches double figures.

The mean probability of the favourites winning a race, for the purpose of Table 2-2 and Table 2-3, was calculated as follows:

For each race, the odds for the first three in the betting was converted to probabilities using the formula 1 divided by the odds +1 (for example: 4/1=1 divided by 4+1=1/5=0.20. The first three in the betting could be first, second and third favourite, favourite and joint second favourites, or three co-favourites etc. In cases, for example, where there was a favourite, second favourite and three co-third favourites would be taken into account.

In most cases (531 races) only three horses were used, four horses were needed in 71 races and five horses were taken in account in 12 races. The sum of the probabilities of the favourites (three, four and five horses) was then expressed as a percentage of the total margin, and this percentage was reduced to a probability, where the percentage was expressed as a fraction of 1.

The betting margin itself was deemed not to matter using the assumption that all horses made a contribution towards the overall margin in favour of the bookmakers in the same proportion as the relative probabilities would indicate. In races of four or more runners, the probability of one of the favourites winning ranged from near certainty (0.983) to highly uncertain, due to the competitive nature of the race (0.202). The lowest probability where one of the favourites won was close to the lowest mark at 0.232, while the highest defeated probability was 0.925. Here, in a four-runner race at Carlisle on June 26 they bet 10/11, 3/1 twice but the outsider at 11/1 won the race by a comfortable length.

series of races. The *Raceform on Saturday* punter would receive £33.60 twenty-five times, while the *Newspaper Mash* punter would receive £840 just once.

Assuming the results were unbiased, meaning that in the long term the actual results were consistent with the market odds (as illustrated above, to be consistent with Shin's views) then the sum of the Tote dividends would exactly equal the Expected Value, which would be the total value of the pool, less the percentage deduction made. This is shown in Table 2-4 in the column headed 'Unbiased results'.

If the actual results were not unbiased, but more favourites won than the market odds would imply, then the sum of the dividends paid would be less than the Expected Value. This is shown in Table 2-4 in the column headed 'Favourites favoured'. On the other hand, if outsiders were favoured, then the sum of the dividends paid would be more than the expected value. This is shown in the column headed 'Outsiders favoured'.

Another way of looking at this is to imagine that £10 was staked on every horse in an eleven runner race, where the betting margin was 119.2, equal to the Tote deduction of 16 per cent. If the 2/1 favourite (excluding stake) won the race, then £80 would be lost, while if a 20/1 outsider (again, excluding stake) won, a profit of £100 would be made. Overall, in 100 races, from a total stake of £11,000, the expected return would be £9,240. However, if the favourite won every race the total return would be a mere £3,000, while the outsider winning every race would yield £21,000. Given the Tote deducts 16 per cent, a total yield less than £9,240 would indicate a favourite bias, while a total yield in excess of this figure would indicate an outsider bias.

-In the next theoretical market (Table 2-5) there is an eleven-runner race and an eighteen-runner race. The market is for bookmakers and the starting assumption is that the process will commence with modification of the true odds to allow a standard margin of 1.5 per cent per runner. Note that this gives an overall margin lower than the Tote (always a fixed 119.0476 per race, assuming the 16 per cent deduction is maintained) in the eleven-runner race, but higher overall margin when compared with the Tote in the eighteen-runner race.

A significant problem for the bookmaker is that in the eleven-runner race one of the two rank outsiders may (remember *may*, not will) be the subject of an insider trading coup and he may be the one to end up skint and suffering in silence. He cannot afford to take the risk and his only option is to shorten the price of the two outsiders. This is illustrated in the top half of Table 2.5 and as can be seen, the effect of reducing the risk of an insider trading attack is to increase the margin per runner from 1.52 % to 2.21%..

The problems are even greater in the eighteen-runner race with four horses at long odds and a further four horses at massive odds, based on the true probabilities. Unlike the Tote, where an insider trading attack would merely reduce the dividend, assuming the chosen horse won, the bookmaker is potentially vulnerable. This time reducing outsiders' odds to manageable levels has the effect of increasing the margin per runner from 1.53% to 2.47%.

Clearly such action would make the bookmaker uncompetitive with the Tote and accordingly further adjustments have to be made to appear competitive. The second stage in the process is the principle where the odds are harmonised (or compressed) to limit the impact of potential insider trading. This is illustrated in Table 2-6. The starting point is that the probability of winning for each horse is identical to Table 2-4. The next step in this table is to adjust these probabilities to give the bookmaker an identical margin to that taken by the Tote. This is shown as 'Probability with margin' and is calculated on each line by multiplying the probability by 1.192. These 'probabilities with margin' are then converted to odds and are shown in the column headed 'Equivalent odds'.

At this stage, if these odds were offered by the bookmaker, then the outcome would be exactly the same as illustrated for the Tote (Table 2-4). If every horse in the race was backed for a £10 stake in 100 races and the results were unbiased then the £11,000 investment would yield £9,240. A 20% bias towards the favourites would yield £7,551 in total, while a 20% bias towards the outsiders would yield £10,929 in total.

To harmonise the probabilities, a probability factor is added to each outsider to reduce the odds to the desired level and equivalent probability factors are deducted from the favourites. In Table 2-6 this is shown in the column 'Harmonising probabilities'. Note that the sum of these probabilities adds to zero, so that the betting margin has been maintained. The effect of harmonising the

18

probabilities is that outsiders' odds are reduced significantly, but the favourites' odds are only increased slightly. At the favourite end of the spectrum, 9/4 becomes 11/4, 100/30 becomes 4/1, 9/2 becomes 11/2, 15/2 becomes 17/2, 10/1 becomes 11/1, but at the outsider end of the spectrum 100/1 is down to 33/1, 40/1 is down to 20/1, 25/1 is down to 16/1, and 20/1 and 16/1 are both reduced to 12/1. What has happened is that the spread of odds has been compressed. As can be seen from Table 2-6, the effect of odds' harmonisation is to reduce liabilities whether or not the results are unbiased or there is a 20% bias in any direction.

If this harmonisation hypothesis is to stand up to test, then based on the analysis of the June 1996 results there would be no effect in Grade A races and there would be little effect in races where the number of runners was in single figures.

Of course, the effect of the odds' harmonisation as demonstrated is based on an equal amount being placed on each horse in the race. In a real situation, more money would be placed on the favourite than on the second favourite and so on down to the outsiders. Taking this into account, the financial effect of harmonisation should disappear, so the end result would be that bookmakers would achieve a net margin similar to that of the Tote, but the benefit would be that risk of effective attack from inside traders would be eliminated at zero or minimal cost.

The next step was to test this hypothesis with real data.

2.4 Methodology and Results

A limitation of previous academic models evaluating the betting market has been the size of the data set. Williams and Paton (1997), in recognising this, carried out a much larger survey than previously attempted taking in 5,903 horses running in 510 races. By evaluating all full meetings run on turf between 19 March 1992 and 18 May 1992 they took in every type of race, but could not take account of seasonal variations. For example, experienced punters know that many more favourites win in high summer, when form has bedded down and the going is consistent, than in the spring, when the new season's form has not become established, or in the autumn when form is disrupted by changes in going. Accordingly, any data set should take in a full season.

Races are staged with the objective of matching the grade of race to the horse population, so that a full analysis (accounting for every race run) drawn graphically would look like a normal distribution, with grade D races representing the peak and grade A races and grade F/G races at each outer edge. However, with previous analysis indicating that grade A and B races attracted lower betting margins than the rest, the objective was to ensure that a significant number of these races were represented.

The conclusion was that any analysis would have to encompass two complete seasons and that the full spectrum of races would have to be included. For this reason, the first three racecourses chosen were Doncaster, Epsom and Newmarket, to ensure all classics were covered. Next, Ascot and York were chosen because of the high quality of racing staged and finally Goodwood and Newbury were chosen as they staged a reasonable number of average races, together with better quality racing.

The races covered over two seasons at these seven racecourses are shown in Table 2-7. In all, 18,923 runners were analyzed, running in 1,653 races, an overall average of 11.45 per race.

The primary objective of the exercise was to see if the favourite/longshot bias disappeared, when the values were determined by Tote prices and the secondary objective was to try to develop a method of predicting whether the starting price or Tote dividend would give the better result in particular circumstances.

Each race was analysed and every horse was put into one of six positions, based on their starting prices:

(1) The favourite was the lowest priced horse, whether individually or jointly.

(2) The second favourite was the horse whose price indicated that only one other horse in the race had a lower price. It was possible to have joint or co second favourites, but there could not be a second favourite if there were joint or co favourites in the race.

(3) The third favourite was the horse whose price indicated that only two other horses in the race had a lower price. It was possible to have joint or co third favourites, but there could not be a third favourite if there were co favourites in the race, or two favourites and one second favourite, or one favourite and two joint second favourites etc.

Table 2-4 Calculation of theoretical betting market and effect on punters
(Tote betting)

Horse Number	Horse	Chance of winning	Probability	Tote Dividend £1 stake
1	Raceform on Saturday	25 in 100	0.250	3.36
2	Think Twice	20 in 100	0.200	4.20
3	Heavy Humour	15 in 100	0.150	5.60
4	Easily Third	10 in 100	0.100	8.40
5	Brassed Off	8 in 100	0.080	10.50
6	Embarrassed	7 in 100	0.070	12.00
7	Suitable Lesson	5 in 100	0.050	16.80
8	Tudor Prince	4 in 100	0.040	21.00
9	Sporting Price	3 in 100	0.030	28.00
10	Racing Rituals	2 in 100	0.020	42.00
11	Newpaper Mash	1 in 100	0.010	84.00
			1.000	

Punter stakes £10 on horse in each of 100 races (= £11,000 staked in total)

Horse Number	Horse	Return if wins (£)	Unbiased results		Favourites favoured		Outsiders favoured	
			Number of wins	Total Returns (£)	Number of wins	Total Returns (£)	Number of wins	Total Returns (£)
1	Raceform on Saturday	33.60	25	840	30	1,008	20	672
2	Think Twice	42.00	20	840	22	924	18	756
3	Heavy Humour	56.00	15	840	17	952	13	728
4	Easily Third	84.00	10	840	10	840	10	840
5	Brassed Off	105.00	8	840	5	525	11	1,155
6	Embarrassed	120.00	7	840	5	600	9	1,080
7	Suitable Lesson	168.00	5	840	4	672	6	1,008
8	Tudor Prince	210.00	4	840	3	630	5	1,050
9	Sporting Price	280.00	3	840	2	560	4	1,120
10	Racing Rituals	420.00	2	840	2	840	2	840
11	Newpaper Mash	840.00	1	840	0	0	2	1,680
			100	9,240	100	7,551	100	10,929

Total stake = £11,000. Tote take out 16%. Expected return with no bias = £11,000 x 0.84 = £9,240

Table 2-5(i) Calculation of effect on betting margins, by shortening outsiders (Eleven runner race)

Horse Number	Horse	Probability with standard margin	Equivalent Odds	Odds with Outsiders' Odds Shortened	Revised odds converted to probabilities
1	Willie Win	0.200	4/1	4/1	0.200
2	Insurance For Me	0.167	5/1	5/1	0.167
3	Smooth Operator	0.125	7/1	7/1	0.125
4	Easily Led	0.118	15/2	15/2	0.118
5	Brave Backer	0.111	8/1	8/1	0.111
6	Oh So Slow	0.111	8/1	8/1	0.111
7	Old Custom	0.105	17/2	17/2	0.105
8	Klever Speller	0.100	9/1	9/1	0.100
9	Investment Of Faith	0.091	10/1	10/1	0.091
10	End Up Skint	0.029	33/1	14/1	0.067
11	Silent Suffering	0.010	100/1	20/1	0.048
		1.167			1.243
	Margin per runner	1.52			2.21

Note: Standard margin is taken to be 1.5% per runner. There is a slight difference (1.52 against 1.50) due to the constraint of matching probabilities with odds for illustrative purposes. Same applies to Table 2-5 (ii)

Table 2-5(ii) Calculation of effect on betting margins, by shortening outsiders (Eighteen runner race)

Horse Number	Horse	Probability with standard margin	Equivalent Odds	Odds with Outsiders' Odds Shortened	Revised odds converted to probabilities
1	Willie Win	0.200	4/1	4/1	0.200
2	Insurance For Me	0.167	5/1	5/1	0.167
3	Smooth Operator	0.133	13/2	13/2	0.133
4	Easily Led	0.125	7/1	7/1	0.125
5	Brave Backer	0.111	8/1	8/1	0.111
6	Oh So Slow	0.091	10/1	9/1	0.100
7	Old Custom	0.083	11/1	10/1	0.091
8	Klever Speller	0.077	12/1	11/1	0.083
9	Investment Of Faith	0.067	14/1	12/1	0.077
10	End Up Skint	0.059	16/1	14/1	0.067
11	Silent Suffering	0.048	20/1	16/1	0.059
12	Courageous Client	0.038	25/1	20/1	0.048
13	Undesirable Understudy	0.029	33/1	25/1	0.038
14	Trot Along	0.020	50/1	33/1	0.029
15	Oranges And Lemons	0.013	75/1	33/1	0.029
16	Dangerous Accumulator	0.010	100/1	33/1	0.029
17	Deadly Lottery	0.004	250/1	33/1	0.029
18	Seventeen Sisters	0.002	500/1	33/1	0.029
		1.277			1.444
	Margin per runner	1.53			2.47

21

(4) The fourth favourite was the horse whose price indicated that only three other horses in the race had a lower price. It was possible to have joint or co fourth favourites, but there could not be a fourth favourite if four or more horses had been classified first, second or third favourites.

(5) All horses, not classified as first, second, third or fourth favourite, with a starting price no greater than 14/1 was designated to be fifth favourite.

(6) All horses with a starting price greater than 14/1, irrespective of their position in the market, was classified as sixth favourite.

For example, in the Stanley Racing Summer Stakes at York on July 10 1998 they bet: 5/6, 7/1 twice, 8/1 twice, 9/1 and 33/1. This betting would be classified as follows:

Favourite 1
Second favourite 2
Third favourite 0
Fourth favourite 2
Fifth favourite 1
Sixth favourite 1
Total 7 runners

As the winner was the 9/1 chance, the winner would be designated 'fifth' favourite.

The betting margin on the race was recorded (114.7), the margin per runner calculated (2.10), the grade was noted (A) and the starting price dividend, including return of stake, to a £10 stake was calculated (£100), together with the Tote dividend, paying £9.40 (£94) to the same £10 stake.

The point was that although horses were placed in order based on their starting prices, any bias would be calculated from the Tote dividends. For example, if every race run showed the same bias as the above race, then there would be a sixty per cent bias towards outsiders. This is calculated by first multiplying the stakes of £70 (£10 on seven horses) by 0.84 (to take account of the 16% deduction made by the Tote) to give an Expected Value of £58.80. The actual dividend of £94 was sixty per cent higher than this figure.

This process was repeated for the remaining 1,652 races.

Table 2-8 shows the summary results of this analysis, which indicated a good degree of consistency between the two years. The first and most important point to note is that while the favourite/longshot bias is confirmed using starting prices, it disappears when Tote dividends are used. This must mean that the cause of the phenomenon known as favourite/longshot bias is due to the bookmakers harmonizing the odds to limit their risk of an attack from insider traders.

At Tote odds, the bias is calculated to be 0.56% towards the favourites in 1997 and 0.16% towards the longshots in 1998. Given that races, by their very nature uncertain, the evenness or lack of bias is striking. In 1997, irrespective of which band of horse a punter chose to back, the returns would have been very close. Compared to an Expected Value of 84%, the actual returns varied between 78.5% and 88.4%. In 1998, the range of the spread looks to be even smaller, apart form a crossover between the third and fourth favourites.

The prime effect of bookmakers harmonising the odds is that betting patterns emerge, which makes it possible to predict whether the starting price or Tote dividend will give the better return. A review of the full data (Table 2-8) reveals that starting prices usually beat the Tote dividend if the favourite or second favourite wins. The comparison for the third favourite is very close, but in both years the starting price just had the edge. The change comes, with the fourth favourite, where, although the results are variable, overall the Tote dividends win by a small margin.

However, as can be seen from the figures, the real impact of odds' harmonisation is to dramatically reduce the starting prices of those horses not in the first four in the betting and as the position of the horse in the betting goes out, so does the probability of the Tote producing a significantly higher dividend when compared with starting prices.

Table 2-8 clearly shows that the effect of bookmakers' odds harmonisation is that anyone backing every horse with the Tote would achieve a far better result than another backing every horse at starting prices. There are exceptions, of course. There is little evidence, for example, of harmonization in small fields, especially in grade A races with less than ten runners.

At this point, it must be stressed that the calculation of backing every horse in every race is computed for the sole purpose of assessing favourite/longshot bias and is not taken to be repre-

Table 2-6 Calculation of theoretical betting market with 'harmonised' odds, and effect on punters (Betting with bookmakers)

Horse Number	Horse	Chance of winning	Probability	Probability with margin	Eqivalent odds	Harmonizing Probabilities	Revised Probabilities	Final Equiv. odds
1	Raceform on Saturday	25 in 100	0.250	0.298	9/4	(0.035)	0.263	11/4
2	Think Twice	20 in 100	0.200	0.238	100/30	(0.028)	0.210	4/1
3	Heavy Humour	15 in 100	0.150	0.179	9/2	(0.021)	0.158	11/2
4	Easily Third	10 in 100	0.100	0.119	15/2	(0.014)	0.105	17/2
5	Brassed Off	8 in 100	0.080	0.095	10/1	(0.012)	0.083	11/1
6	Embarrassed	7 in 100	0.070	0.083	11/1	0.000	0.083	11/1
7	Suitable Lesson	5 in 100	0.050	0.060	16/1	0.017	0.077	12/1
8	Tudor Prince	4 in 100	0.040	0.048	20/1	0.029	0.077	12/1
9	Sporting Price	3 in 100	0.030	0.036	25/1	0.023	0.059	16/1
10	Racing Rituals	2 in 100	0.020	0.024	40/1	0.024	0.048	20/1
11	Newpaper Mash	1 in 100	0.010	0.012	100/1	0.017	0.029	33/1
			1.000	1.192		(0.000)	1.192	

Punter stakes £10 on horse in each of 100 races (= £11,000 staked in total)

			Unbiased results		Favourites favoured		Outsiders favoured	
Horse Number	Horse	Return if wins (£)	Number of wins	Total Returns (£)	Number of wins	Total Returns (£)	Number of wins	Total Returns (£)
1	Raceform on Saturday	37.50	25	938	30	1,125	20	750
2	Think Twice	50.00	20	1,000	22	1,100	18	900
3	Heavy Humour	65.00	15	975	17	1,105	13	845
4	Easily Third	95.00	10	950	10	950	10	950
5	Brassed Off	120.00	8	960	5	600	11	1,320
6	Embarrassed	120.00	7	840	5	600	9	1,080
7	Suitable Lesson	130.00	5	650	4	520	6	780
8	Tudor Prince	130.00	4	520	3	390	5	650
9	Sporting Price	170.00	3	510	2	340	4	680
10	Racing Rituals	210.00	2	420	2	420	2	420
11	Newpaper Mash	340.00	1	340	0	0	2	680
			100	8,103	100	7,150	100	9,055

Total stake = £11,000. Margins taken (19.05 divided by 119.05 = 16.0%, same as Tote) imply an Expected Return with no bias of £9,240, but effect of harmonization is to reduce liabilities, even though overall margin is maintained.

Table 2-7   The data set

(Races analysed to assess state of the betting market in 1997)

1997	Total number of races	Grade of race						
		A	B	C	D	E	F	G
Ascot	84	31	25	14	12	2	0	0
Doncaster	132	16	12	32	48	19	4	1
Epsom	59	10	6	18	18	7	0	0
Goodwood	130	21	12	29	52	16	0	0
Newbury	109	21	17	27	39	4	1	0
Newmarket	226	47	23	52	81	19	2	2
York	87	19	24	19	19	5	1	0
Total - seven racecourses	827	165	119	191	269	72	8	3

(Races analysed to assess state of the betting market in 1998)

1998	Total number of races	Grade of race						
		A	B	C	D	E	F	G
Ascot	84	30	25	15	13	1	0	0
Doncaster	135	16	17	29	50	17	6	0
Epsom	58	10	6	14	21	7	0	0
Goodwood	130	22	10	31	49	18	0	0
Newbury	94	19	18	22	29	4	2	0
Newmarket	225	52	26	46	76	21	2	2
York	100	21	26	20	25	8	0	0
Total - seven racecourses	826	170	128	177	263	76	10	2

sentative of actual racing patterns. For this purpose, it is assumed that betting with bookmakers is consistent with the overall probabilities, so, for example, much more would be bet on the favourite, when compared with outsiders. A estimation of bookmakers' profitability is made on this basis (Table 2-9). This estimate suggests that bookmakers pay back to punters a slightly higher percentage overall than the Tote and that the cost of implementing their harmonisation strategy is about one and a half percentage points.

Given the consistency of betting patterns between starting prices and Tote dividends, it is possible, through major variations in expectation, to have a very good idea of when insider trading is actually taking place. The impact on the market of insider trading can be divided into two categories:

(1) The superior knowledge of the insider trader gives an advantage over the ordinary punter, but the resultant bets are not close to being risk free. Such insider trading is detected by inflated betting margins, where the margin will be over 2.5% per runner. In these cases, the probability of the winner being in the first four in the betting increases from the average of 0.7 to 0.8, but detection is difficult prior to the race.

This type of insider trading takes place in just under 20% of races and appears to be on the increase (see Table 3-2, in chapter 3), possibly justifying bookmakers' concerns.

(2) The superior knowledge is such that a significant advantage can be achieved and the risks are much less than those associated with category (1). This insider trading is detected by certain race types (see chapter 3) and can be detected prior to the race as the Tote odds will be significantly higher than the bookmakers' odds. The estimate is that this type of insider trading takes place in approximately 1.5% of all races This figure would imply that the cost of insurance in respect of insider trading would be just about equal the potential claims. However, if bookmakers discontinued the odds harmonisation strategy there would be little difference between them and the Tote.

Table 2-10 shows the results from the seven racecourses analysed by grade of race. There appears to be a slight bias towards the favourites in grade D races (probably due to scouts' involvement with higher class maiden races), and a more significant bias towards longshots in grade E to G races (probably due to the difficulty of properly assessing poor form). Table 2-11 shows the results from the seven racecourses analysed by betting margin. As can be seen by comparing the Tote returns with the starting price returns, the apparent effect of bookmakers' odds harmonisation is very high. What is happening in some of these races is that the prices of the outsiders are being cut back as the first stage in the harmonisation process, but the prices of the favourites are not going out, due to insider trading, and it is this combination which is forcing the betting margins to go out.

In respect of analysis by betting margin, it is noticeable that in very low margin races there is an indication of bias towards the favourites and in races where margins are just above the mean the indication of bias in the opposite direction, towards the outsiders. However, the races with the very highest margins produce variable results. The conclusion from this is that while ordinary punters may feel confident to back one of the favourites in low margin races, they should not be confident to do so in very high margin races, as although there is a probability of 0.8 that one of the first four favourites will win the race, it is also likely that the bookmakers' odds would have been cut to the point that it was impossible to achieve value.

Table 2-12 gives examples of type 2 insider trading. The conclusion drawn from this table is that three variables, the number of runners, type 2 insider trading and the grade of race explain over 75% of the variables of the betting margin. Type 1 insider trading will explain at least part of the remaining 25% of the variables not covered by this analysis.

Tables 2-13 through to 2-19 give an analysis of betting returns, by racecourse.

Summary

The favourite/longshot bias phenomenon is explained by bookmakers harmonising the odds to reduce the risk of potential, not actual, insider trading. The proof of this is that bias at Tote odds is not detectable. Accordingly, actual results in the long tem are consistent with the odds, indicated by their order, as determined by the market makers. Further, in a test, using starting prices, taking in all races run in June 1996, there was found to be no bias in grade A races and very little bias

Table 2-8 Analysis of betting returns - seven racecourses (Ascot, Doncaster, Epsom, Goodwood, Newbury, Newmarket and York)

Betting returns based on placing £10 win on every horse that ran (Rule 4 has been applied to starting price returns, where appropriate)

Returns in 1997	Number of runners	Number of winners	Winning percentage	Total stake (£10 unit) £p	SP returns £p	Profit/(loss) £p	Percentage returned (%)	Tote returns £p	Profit/(loss) £p	Percentage returned (%)
Favourite	921	272	29.5	9,210.00	8,502.79	(707.21)	92.3	8,140.00	(1,070.00)	88.4
Second favourite	901	154.5	17.1	9,010.00	8,089.65	(920.35)	89.8	7,796.00	(1,214.00)	86.5
Third favourite	844	107	12.7	8,440.00	7,401.00	(1,039.00)	87.7	7,386.00	(1,054.00)	87.5
Fourth favourite	815	79	9.7	8,150.00	6,746.75	(1,403.25)	82.8	7,011.00	(1,139.00)	86.0
Others - odds up to 14/1	2,191	130.5	6.0	21,910.00	14,765.00	(7,145.00)	67.4	17,209.00	(4,701.00)	78.5
Others - odds 16/1 and higher	3,669	84	2.3	36,690.00	19,930.00	(16,760.00)	54.3	30,482.00	(6,208.00)	83.1
All	9,341	827	8.9	93,410.00	65,435.19	(27,974.81)	70.1	78,024.00	(15,386.00)	83.5

	Average number of runners	Average margin per runner (%)	Overall betting margin	(Favourite/longshot bias (%))	Total stake (£)	Expected return (£)	Effect of Fav/Long bias (£)	Harmonization effect (£)	Actual return (£)
Bookmakers	11.30	2.03	122.9390	(0.56)	93,410	75,981	(425)	(10,121)	65,435
Tote	11.30	1.69	119.0476	(0.56)	93,410	78,464	(440)	0	78,024

Returns in 1998	Number of runners	Number of winners	Winning percentage	Total stake (£10 unit) £p	SP returns £p	Profit/(loss) £p	Percentage returned (%)	Tote returns £p	Profit/(loss) £p	Percentage returned (%)
Favourite	927	266	28.7	9,270.00	8,633.76	(636.24)	93.1	8,229.00	(1,041.00)	88.8
Second favourite	899	162.5	18.1	8,990.00	8,455.15	(534.85)	94.1	8,033.00	(957.00)	89.4
Third favourite	833	82.5	9.9	8,330.00	5,631.33	(2,698.67)	67.6	5,561.00	(2,769.00)	66.8
Fourth favourite	792	82	10.4	7,920.00	6,845.00	(1,075.00)	86.4	7,209.00	(711.00)	91.0
Others - odds up to 14/1	2,363	140	5.9	23,630.00	16,069.00	(7,561.00)	68.0	19,883.00	(3,747.00)	84.1
Others - odds 16/1 and higher	3,768	93	2.5	37,680.00	22,234.50	(15,445.50)	59.0	31,716.00	(5,964.00)	84.2
All	9,582	826	8.6	95,820.00	67,868.74	(27,951.26)	70.8	80,631.00	(15,189.00)	84.1

	Average number of runners	Average margin per runner (%)	Overall betting margin	(Favourite/longshot bias (%))	Total stake (£)	Expected return (£)	Effect of Fav/Long bias (£)	Harmonization effect (£)	Actual return (£)
Bookmakers	11.60	2.07	124.0120	0.18	95,820	77,267	139	(9,537)	67,869
Tote	11.60	1.64	119.0476	0.18	95,820	80,489	142	0	80,631

Note: Where the number of winners shown includes one-half, this indicates one dead-heat in each year

in races where the runners were in single figures.

The explanations for these results are that bookmakers do not harmonize odds in classics, nor is there much evidence that they do so in other grade A races, especially as such races generally attract small fields (average number of runners per race 8.72 in 1997 and 8.45 in 1998, for seven racecourses, compared with overall average of 11.30 and 11.60 runners per race respectively). The need to harmonise the odds is proportional to the number of runners, as the number of favourites remain static, while the number of outsiders increase as the size of the field increases.

Two examples illustrate the point. In the 1998 Sagitta 2000 Guineas Stakes (classic) they bet: 10/11, 7/2. 8/1, 14/1, 16/1 twice, 25/1, 28/1, 33/1, 40/1 twice, 75/1, 100/1 three times, 200/1 twice and 500/1 (18 runners, betting margin 124.7). On the same day as this classic was run, in the 18 runner Thirsk Hunt Cup Handicap (Class C) they bet: 100/30, 6/1, 7/1, 8/1 twice, 9/1, 10/1, 11/1, 20/1 twice, 25/1 twice, 33/1 four times and 50/1 twice.

Although odds' harmonisation allows long odds to shorten disproportionately to short odds lengthening, occasional influences such as actual, rather than perceived, insider trading restrict extension and this sometimes forces the betting margin to go out. Hence, the prime influence on betting margins is the number of runners, caused by both perceived and actual insider trading. Additionally, other forms of insider trading and the grade of race have an influence on the final betting margin.

In theory, it might be said that increasing betting margins and odds' harmonization should increase bookmakers' profitability, but the expectation must be that punters' bets would be proportional to the probabilities, so that the most of the bets taken by bookmakers would be at their least favourable margins. Accordingly, one would expect bookmakers' overall margins to be consistent with those of the Tote, although their end result would be dependent upon their ability to balance the books and the degree of risk they find acceptable in an effort to make better than average profits.

Knowledge of the market is an important weapon in punters' armoury and how such knowledge can be exploited is discussed in the next chapter.

References

Box, G.E.P. (1976). 'Science and Statistics'. *Journal of American Statistical Association*, vol.71, no.356, December.

Crafts, N.F.R. (1985). 'Some evidence of insider knowledge in horse race betting in Britain'. *Economics*, vol.52, pp.295-304

Jockey Club Committee of Inquiry (1968). *The Racing Industry* Trustees of the Jockey Club.

Jullien B and Salanie B (1994). 'Measuring the incidence of insider trading: a comment on Shin'. *Economic Journal*, vol.104, pp 1418-9.

Shin, H.S. (1991). 'Optimal betting odds against insider traders'. *Economic Journal*, vol.101, pp 1179-85

Shin, H.S. (1992). 'Prices of state contingent claims with insider traders, and the favourite-longshot bias'. *Economic Journal*, vol.102, pp 426-35

Shin, H.S. (1993). 'Measuring the incidence of insider trading in a market for state contingent claims'. *Economic Journal*, vol.103, pp 1141-53.

Williams, L.V and Paton, D (1997). 'Why is there favourite-longshot bias in British racetrack betting markets?' *Economic Journal*, vol.107, pp 150-8.

Table 2-9 Estimate of margin achieved by bookmakers and Tote at seven racecourses

(Assuming total stakes, as shown in Table 2-9)

1997	Percentage of stake #	Stake £	Percentage returned	Returns £
Favourite	37.41	34,945	92.3	32,254
Second favourite	22.19	20,728	89.8	18,614
Third favourite	16.22	15,151	87.7	13,287
Fourth favourite	12.61	11,779	82.8	9,753
Others - odds up to 14/1	8.48	7,921	67.4	5,339
Others - odds 16/1 and higher	3.09	2,886	54.3	1,567
Total	100.00	93,410	70.1	80,814

Bookmakers' estimated percentage of stakes paid out   86.5

Tote's actual percentage of stakes paid out   84.0

1998	Percentage of stake #	Stake £	Percentage returned	Returns £
Favourite	36.43	34,907	93.1	32,498
Second favourite	22.80	21,847	94.1	20,558
Third favourite	16.72	16,021	67.6	10,830
Fourth favourite	12.82	12,284	86.4	10,613
Others - odds up to 14/1	7.93	7,599	68.0	5,167
Others - odds 16/1 and higher	3.30	3,162	59.0	1,866
Total	100.00	95,820	70.8	81,532

Bookmakers' estimated percentage of stakes paid out   85.1

Tote's actual percentage of stakes paid out   84.0

 # The percentage stake is estimated from the Tote returns to eliminate the effect of harmonization

These figures suggest bookmakers pay out about one and a half more percentage points than the Tote, if there is no 'real' favourite/longshot bias. Because of odds harmonization, bookmakers will pay more than this when there is a 'real' slight favourite bias and less than this when there is a 'real' slight longshot bias.

The implication of this difference of one and a half percentage points is the cost to bookmakers of taking protective action against 'insider trading'. Interestingly, it is estimated that approximately 1.5% of all races run are subject to insider trading to the extent that such insider trading has an impact on the market.

Table 2-10 Analysis of betting returns - seven racecourses (Ascot, Doncaster, Epsom, Goodwood, Newbury, Newmarket and York)

Betting returns based on placing £10 win on every horse that ran (Rule 4 has been applied to starting price returns, where appropriate)

Returns in 1997	Average number of runners	Average margin per runner (%)	Overall betting margin	(Favourite/ longshot bias (%)	Total stake (£)	Expected return (£)	Effect of Fav/Long bias (£)	Harmonization effect (£)	Actual return (£)	Percentage returned (%)
Bookmakers (All races)	11.30	2.03	122.9390	(0.56)	93,410	75,981	(425)	(10,121)	65,435	70.1
Tote (All races)	11.30	1.69	119.0476	(0.56)	93,410	78,464	(440)	0	78,024	83.5
Bookmakers (Grade A races)	8.72	1.83	115.9576	(5.66)	14,380	12,401	(702)	245	11,944	83.1
Tote (Grade A races)	8.72	2.18	119.0476	(5.66)	14,380	12,079	(684)	0	11,395	79.2
Bookmakers (Grade B races)	13.30	1.92	125.5360	1.98	15,830	12,610	249	(1,586)	11,273	71.2
Tote (Grade B races)	13.30	1.43	119.0476	1.98	15,830	13,297	263	0	13,560	85.7
Bookmakers (Grade C races)	11.58	2.02	123.3916	4.77	22,120	17,927	856	(3,265)	15,518	70.2
Tote (Grade C races)	11.58	1.64	119.0476	4.77	22,120	18,581	887	0	19,468	88.0
Bookmakers (Grade D races)	11.16	2.17	124.2172	(5.57)	30,030	24,175	(1,347)	(3,221)	19,607	65.3
Tote (Grade D races)	11.16	1.71	119.0476	(5.57)	30,030	25,225	(1,406)	0	23,819	79.3
Bookmakers (Grade E to G races)	13.31	2.20	129.2820	5.39	11,050	8,547	460	(1,914)	7,093	64.2
Tote (Grade E to G races)	13.31	1.43	119.0476	5.39	11,050	9,282	500	0	9,782	88.5

Returns in 1998	Average number of runners	Average margin per runner (%)	Overall betting margin	(Favourite/ longshot bias (%)	Total stake (£)	Expected return (£)	Effect of Fav/Long bias (£)	Harmonization effect (£)	Actual return (£)	Percentage returned (%)
Bookmakers (All races)	11.60	2.07	124.0120	0.18	95,820	77,267	136	(9,534)	67,869	70.8
Tote (All races)	11.60	1.64	119.0476	0.18	95,820	80,489	142	0	80,631	84.1
Bookmakers (Grade A races)	8.45	1.91	116.1395	2.56	14,360	12,364	317	(983)	11,698	81.5
Tote (Grade A races)	8.45	2.25	119.0476	2.56	14,360	12,062	309	0	12,371	86.1
Bookmakers (Grade B races)	13.30	1.92	125.5360	(5.81)	17,020	13,558	(787)	(1,133)	11,638	68.4
Tote (Grade B races)	13.30	1.43	119.0476	(5.81)	17,020	14,297	(830)	0	13,467	79.1
Bookmakers (Grade C races)	11.71	2.02	123.6542	(4.71)	20,720	16,756	(789)	(1,071)	14,896	71.9
Tote (Grade C races)	11.71	1.63	119.0476	(4.71)	20,720	17,405	(820)	0	16,585	80.0
Bookmakers (Grade D races)	11.79	2.22	126.1738	(1.90)	31,020	24,585	(467)	(3,172)	20,946	67.5
Tote (Grade D races)	11.79	1.62	119.0476	(1.90)	31,020	26,057	(495)	0	25,562	82.4
Bookmakers (Grade E to G races)	14.43	2.24	132.3232	18.54	12,700	9,598	1,780	(2,687)	8,691	68.4
Tote (Grade E to G races)	14.43	1.32	119.0476	18.54	12,700	10,668	1,978	0	12,646	99.6

Table 2-11 Analysis of betting returns – seven racecourses (Ascot, Doncaster, Epsom, Goodwood, Newbury, Newmarket and York)

Betting returns based on placing £10 win on every horse that ran (Rule 4 has been applied to starting price returns, where appropriate)

Returns in 1997	Average number of runners	Average margin per runner (%)	Overall betting margin	(Favourite/ longshot bias (%)	Total stake (£)	Expected return (£)	Effect of Fav/Long bias (£)	Harmonization effect (£)	Actual return (£)	Percentage returned (%)
Bookmakers (All races)	11.30	2.03	122.9390	(0.56)	93,410	75,981	(425)	(10,121)	65,435	70.1
Tote (All races)	11.30	1.69	119.0476	(0.56)	93,410	78,464	(440)	0	78,024	83.5
Books (margins up to 1.5% per runner)	11.49	1.30	114.9370	(3.79)	18,960	16,496	(625)	(1,709)	14,162	74.7
Tote (as above)	11.49	1.66	119.0476	(3.79)	18,960	15,926	(603)	0	15,323	80.8
Books (margins 1.51% to 2.00%)	11.75	1.80	121.1500	(4.63)	37,950	31,325	(1,450)	(2,681)	27,194	71.7
Tote (as above)	11.75	1.62	119.0476	(4.63)	37,950	31,878	(1,476)	0	30,402	80.1
Books (margins 2.01% to 2.50%)	11.39	2.27	125.8553	4.60	22,090	17,552	807	(3,554)	14,805	67.0
Tote (as above)	11.39	1.67	119.0476	4.60	22,090	18,556	853	0	19,409	87.9
Books (margins 2.51% and above)	9.94	3.07	130.5158	6.49	14,410	11,041	717	(2,484)	9,274	64.4
Tote (as above)	9.94	1.92	119.0476	6.49	14,410	12,104	786	0	12,890	89.5

Returns in 1998	Average number of runners	Average margin per runner (%)	Overall betting margin	(Favourite/ longshot bias (%)	Total stake (£)	Expected return (£)	Effect of Fav/Long bias (£)	Harmonization effect (£)	Actual return (£)	Percentage returned (%)
Bookmakers (All races)	11.60	2.07	124.0120	0.18	95,820	77,267	136	(9,534)	67,869	70.8
Tote (All races)	11.60	1.64	119.0476	0.18	95,820	80,489	142	0	80,631	84.1
Books (margins up to 1.5% per runner)	11.53	1.30	114.9890	(15.14)	15,680	13,636	(2,064)	(948)	10,624	67.8
Tote (as above)	11.53	1.65	119.0476	(15.14)	15,680	13,171	(1,994)	0	11,177	71.3
Books (margins 1.51% to 2.00%)	12.37	1.77	121.8949	5.14	35,390	29,033	1,492	(3,638)	26,887	76.0
Tote (as above)	12.37	1.54	119.0476	5.14	35,390	29,728	1,528	0	31,256	88.3
Books (margins 2.01% to 2.50%)	11.94	2.23	126.6262	6.19	29,500	23,297	1,441	(3,957)	20,781	70.4
Tote (as above)	11.94	1.60	119.0476	6.19	29,500	24,780	1,533	0	26,313	89.2
Books (margins 2.51% and above)	9.71	3.03	129.4213	(7.22)	15,250	11,783	(851)	(1,355)	9,577	62.8
Tote (as above)	9.71	1.96	119.0476	(7.22)	15,250	12,810	(925)	0	11,885	77.9

Table 2-12 Comparison between betting margins — 1998 (Evidence of Insider Trading and race grade)

Race number as Form Book (1998)	Winner	Grade of race	Starting price (to £10 stake)	Tote dividends expected (based on bet. pos(£10 stake)	Actual Tote dividends (to £10 stake)	Betting margin per runner	Average betting margin per runner for race grade	Variance per runner
1772	BAY OF THE ISLANDS	C	64.00	79.00	168.00	7.91	2.02	5.89
3970	CLUNIE	F	70.00	69.00	115.00	2.34	2.24	0.10
1411	DAAWE	D	90.00	111.00	131.00	2.76	2.22	0.54
2313	DEHOUSH	D	110.00	136.00	172.00	3.06	2.22	0.84
2058	GREEK PALACE	B	100.00	95.00	165.00	1.96	1.92	0.04
2935	HIT THE BEACH	D	45.00	44.00	69.00	3.42	2.22	1.20
4318	HOUSTON TIME	D	130.00	161.00	231.00	1.68	2.22	(0.54)
2240	KWELLO	D	90.00	111.00	140.00	2.21	2.22	(0.01)
1744	LADY ANGHARAD	A	120.00	148.00	172.00	0.76	1.91	(1.15)
4357	PARISIEN STAR	C	90.00	95.00	150.00	1.16	2.02	(0.86)
3686	PETROVNA	E	110.00	109.00	173.00	2.33	2.24	0.09
2958	PREMIER LEAGUE	F	90.00	95.00	141.00	2.68	2.24	0.44
3814	RAIVUE	A	90.00	111.00	168.00	2.95	2.22	0.73
3756	RED PRARIE	D	65.00	68.00	107.00	2.09	1.91	0.18
1792	ROSE OF MOONCOIN	D	110.00	116.00	217.00	4.34	2.22	2.12
4066	ROYAL RESULT	D	130.00	161.00	277.00	2.40	2.22	0.18
4513	SILKEN DALLIANCE	B	110.00	105.00	164.00	1.48	1.92	(0.44)
1370	SUNSET HARBOUR	D	85.00	84.00	131.00	1.96	2.22	(0.26)
3021	SWYNFORD DREAM	D	90.00	95.00	131.00	2.02	2.22	(0.20)
4746	UNDETERRED	A	150.00	186.00	489.00	2.12	1.91	0.21
714	YORKIES BOY	A	90.00	111.00	158.00	1.51	1.91	(0.40)

Note: Thirteen of the above races were included in the 1998 analysis of 826 races (see Table 2.9). These thirteen races were included in multiple regression analysis with a dummy variable to indicate "insider trading". The betting margin on the race was found to be well explained by this dummy and the other two variables, the number of runners and the grade of race. These three independent variables explained over 75% of the variation of the betting margin (Adjusted R squared = 0.758).

By far the biggest contributor to the size of the margin was the number of runners and insider trading was found to have slightly more impact than the grade of race. However, there was no correlation between insider trading and the number of runners or insider trading and the grade of race. The conclusion, therefore, is that the relationship between betting margins and the number of runners has little to do with insider trading.

Table 2-13 Analysis of betting returns - Ascot

Betting returns based on placing £10 win on every horse that ran (Rule 4 has been applied to starting price returns, where appropriate)

Returns in 1997	Number of runners	Number of winners	Winning percentage	Total stake (£10 unit) £p	SP returns £p	Profit/(loss) £p	Percentage returned (%)	Tote returns £p	Profit/(loss) £p	Percentage returned (%)
Favourite	95	19	20.0	950.00	732.29	(217.71)	77.1	617.00	(333.00)	64.9
Second favourite	94	17	18.1	940.00	977.50	37.50	104.0	884.00	(56.00)	94.0
Third favourite	82	6	7.3	820.00	475.00	(345.00)	57.9	413.00	(407.00)	50.4
Fourth favourite	84	12	14.3	840.00	1,020.00	180.00	121.4	979.00	139.00	116.5
Others - odds up to 14/1	239	16	6.7	2,390.00	1,755.00	(635.00)	73.4	2,040.00	(350.00)	85.4
Others - odds 16/1 and higher	407	14	3.4	4,070.00	3,360.00	(710.00)	82.6	3,936.00	(134.00)	96.7
All	1,001	84	8.4	10,010.00	8,319.79	(1,690.21)	83.1	8,869.00	(1,141.00)	88.6

	Average number of runners	Average margin per runner (%)	Overall betting margin	(Favourite/ longshot bias (%))	Total stake (£)	Expected return (£)	Effect of Fav/Long bias (£)	Harmonization effect (£)	Actual return (£)
Bookmakers	11.92	1.59	118.9528	5.48	10,010	8,415	461	(556)	8,320
Tote	11.92	1.60	119.0476	5.48	10,010	8,408	461	0	8,869

Returns in 1998	Number of runners	Number of winners	Winning percentage	Total stake (£10 unit) £p	SP returns £p	Profit/(loss) £p	Percentage returned (%)	Tote returns £p	Profit/(loss) £p	Percentage returned (%)
Favourite	97	22	22.7	970.00	906.30	(63.70)	93.4	792.00	(178.00)	81.6
Second favourite	91	19	20.9	910.00	1,029.16	119.16	113.1	1,037.00	127.00	114.0
Third favourite	79	10	12.7	790.00	730.00	(60.00)	92.4	743.00	(47.00)	94.1
Fourth favourite	79	11	13.9	790.00	900.00	110.00	113.9	877.00	87.00	111.0
Others - odds up to 14/1	228	12	5.3	2,280.00	1,425.00	(855.00)	62.5	1,690.00	(590.00)	74.1
Others - odds 16/1 and higher	439	10	2.3	4,390.00	2,250.00	(2,140.00)	51.3	2,305.00	(2,085.00)	52.5
All	1,013	84	8.3	10,130.00	7,240.46	(2,889.54)	71.5	7,444.00	(2,686.00)	73.5

	Average number of runners	Average margin per runner (%)	Overall betting margin	(Favourite/ longshot bias (%))	Total stake (£)	Expected return (£)	Effect of Fav/Long bias (£)	Harmonization effect (£)	Actual return (£)
Bookmakers	12.06	1.63	119.6578	(12.52)	10,130	8,466	(1,060)	(166)	7,240
Tote	12.06	1.58	119.0476	(12.52)	10,130	8,509	(1,065)	0	7,444

Source of data: The Official Form Book (for 1997 and 1998) Raceform

Table 2-14 Analysis of betting returns – Doncaster

Betting returns based on placing £10 win on every horse that ran (Rule 4 has been applied to starting price returns, where appropriate)

Returns in 1997	Number of runners	Number of winners	Winning percentage	Total stake (£10 unit) £p	SP returns £p	Profit/(loss) £p	Percentage returned (%)	Tote returns £p	Profit/(loss) £p	Percentage returned (%)
Favourite	149	36	24.2	1,490.00	1,145.01	(344.99)	76.8	1,095.00	(395.00)	73.5
Second favourite	143	29	20.3	1,430.00	1,604.50	174.50	112.2	1,549.00	119.00	108.3
Third favourite	136	15	11.0	1,360.00	1,105.00	(255.00)	81.3	1,211.00	(149.00)	89.0
Fourth favourite	136	15	11.0	1,360.00	1,307.75	(52.25)	96.2	1,406.00	46.00	103.4
Others - odds up to 14/1	404	25	6.2	4,040.00	2,730.00	(1,310.00)	67.6	3,319.00	(721.00)	82.2
Others - odds 16/1 and higher	646	12	1.9	6,460.00	2,640.00	(3,820.00)	40.9	3,778.00	(2,682.00)	58.5
All	1,614	132	8.2	16,140.00	10,532.26	(5,607.74)	65.3	12,358.00	(3,782.00)	76.6

	Average number of runners	Average margin per runner (%)	Overall betting margin	(Favourite/longshot bias (%))	Total stake (£)	Expected return (£)	Effect of Fav/Long bias (£)	Harmonization effect (£)	Actual return (£)
Bookmakers	12.23	2.20	126.9060	(8.85)	16,140	12,718	(1,126)	(1,060)	10,532
Tote	12.23	1.56	119.0476	(8.85)	16,140	13,558	(1,200)	0	12,358

Returns in 1998	Number of runners	Number of winners	Winning percentage	Total stake (£10 unit) £p	SP returns £p	Profit/(loss) £p	Percentage returned (%)	Tote returns £p	Profit/(loss) £p	Percentage returned (%)
Favourite	153	48	31.4	1,530.00	1,559.11	29.11	101.9	1,503.00	(27.00)	98.2
Second favourite	146	22	15.1	1,460.00	1,075.25	(384.75)	73.6	1,009.00	(451.00)	69.1
Third favourite	142	11	7.7	1,420.00	820.00	(600.00)	57.7	883.00	(537.00)	62.2
Fourth favourite	140	12	8.6	1,400.00	890.00	(510.00)	63.6	859.00	(541.00)	61.4
Others - odds up to 14/1	418	21	5.0	4,180.00	2,269.00	(1,911.00)	54.3	3,230.00	(950.00)	77.3
Others - odds 16/1 and higher	649	21	3.2	6,490.00	4,362.00	(2,128.00)	67.2	6,762.00	272.00	104.2
All	1,648	135	8.2	16,480.00	10,975.36	(5,504.64)	66.6	14,246.00	(2,234.00)	86.4

	Average number of runners	Average margin per runner (%)	Overall betting margin	(Favourite/longshot bias (%))	Total stake (£)	Expected return (£)	Effect of Fav/Long bias (£)	Harmonization effect (£)	Actual return (£)
Bookmakers	12.21	2.37	128.9377	2.91	16,480	12,781	372	(2,178)	10,975
Tote	12.21	1.56	119.0476	2.91	16,480	13,843	403	0	14,246

Source of data: The Official Form Book (for 1997 and 1998) Raceform

Table 2-15 Analysis of betting returns – Epsom (Downs)

Betting returns based on placing £10 win on every horse that ran (Rule 4 has been applied to starting price returns, where appropriate)

Returns in 1997	Number of runners	Number of winners	Winning percentage	Total stake (£10 unit) £p	SP returns £p	Profit/(loss) £p	Percentage returned (%)	Tote returns £p	Profit/(loss) £p	Percentage returned (%)
Favourite	70	22	31.4	700.00	729.56	29.56	104.2	674.00	(26.00)	96.3
Second favourite	58	11	19.0	580.00	557.50	(22.50)	96.1	563.00	(17.00)	97.1
Third favourite	63	12	19.0	630.00	784.00	154.00	124.4	824.00	194.00	130.8
Fourth favourite	61	3	4.9	610.00	203.00	(407.00)	33.3	187.00	(423.00)	30.7
Others - odds up to 14/1	153	9	5.9	1,530.00	975.00	(555.00)	63.7	1,231.00	(299.00)	80.5
Others - odds 16/1 and higher	155	2	1.3	1,550.00	550.00	(1,000.00)	35.5	948.00	(602.00)	61.2
All	560	59	10.5	5,600.00	3,799.06	(1,800.94)	67.8	4,427.00	(1,173.00)	79.1

	Average number of runners	Average margin per runner (%)	Overall betting margin	(Favourite/longshot bias (%)	Total stake (£)	Expected return (£)	Effect of Fav/Long bias (£)	Harmonization effect (£)	Actual return (£)
Bookmakers	9.49	1.80	117.0820	(5.89)	5,600	4,783	(282)	(702)	3,799
Tote	9.49	2.01	119.0476	(5.89)	5,600	4,704	(277)	0	4,427

Returns in 1998	Number of runners	Number of winners	Winning percentage	Total stake (£10 unit) £p	SP returns £p	Profit/(loss) £p	Percentage returned (%)	Tote returns £p	Profit/(loss) £p	Percentage returned (%)
Favourite	64	14	21.9	640.00	430.08	(209.92)	67.2	372.00	(268.00)	58.1
Second favourite	58	14	24.1	580.00	735.83	155.83	126.9	710.00	130.00	122.4
Third favourite	67	5	7.5	670.00	380.00	(290.00)	56.7	357.00	(313.00)	53.3
Fourth favourite	53	6	11.3	530.00	530.00	0.00	100.0	452.00	(78.00)	85.3
Others - odds up to 14/1	169	14	8.3	1,690.00	1,580.00	(110.00)	93.5	1,814.00	124.00	107.3
Others - odds 16/1 and higher	157	5	3.2	1,570.00	1,020.00	(550.00)	65.0	1,209.00	(361.00)	77.0
All	568	58	10.2	5,680.00	4,675.91	(1,004.09)	82.3	4,914.00	(766.00)	86.5

	Average number of runners	Average margin per runner (%)	Overall betting margin	(Favourite/longshot bias (%)	Total stake (£)	Expected return (£)	Effect of Fav/Long bias (£)	Harmonization effect (£)	Actual return (£)
Bookmakers	9.79	1.88	118.4052	3.00	5,680	4,797	144	(265)	4,676
Tote	9.79	1.95	119.0476	3.00	5,680	4,771	143	0	4,914

Source of data: The Official Form Book (for 1997 and 1998) Raceform

Table 2-16 Analysis of betting returns - Goodwood

Betting returns based on placing £10 win on every horse that ran (Rule 4 has been applied to starting price returns, where appropriate)

Returns in 1997	Number of runners	Number of winners	Winning percentage	Total stake (£10 unit) £p	SP returns £p	Profit/(loss) £p	Percentage returned (%)	Tote returns £p	Profit/(loss) £p	Percentage returned (%)
Favourite	146	49	33.6	1,460.00	1,482.38	22.38	101.5	1,479.00	19.00	101.3
Second favourite	141	21	14.9	1,410.00	956.24	(453.76)	67.8	903.00	(507.00)	64.0
Third favourite	129	16	12.4	1,290.00	1,055.00	(235.00)	81.8	1,003.00	(287.00)	77.8
Fourth favourite	125	12	9.6	1,250.00	1,035.00	(215.00)	82.8	1,191.00	(59.00)	95.3
Others - odds up to 14/1	301	19	6.3	3,010.00	2,163.00	(847.00)	71.9	2,397.00	(613.00)	79.6
Others - odds 16/1 and higher	461	13	2.8	4,610.00	2,980.00	(1,630.00)	64.6	3,782.00	(828.00)	82.0
All	1,303	130	10.0	13,030.00	9,671.62	(3,358.38)	74.2	10,755.00	(2,275.00)	82.5

	Average number of runners	Average margin per runner (%)	Overall betting margin	(Favourite)/longshot bias (%)	Total stake (£)	Expected return (£)	Effect of Fav/Long bias (£)	Harmonization effect (£)	Actual return (£)
Bookmakers	10.02	2.00	120.0400	(1.74)	13,030	10,855	(189)	(994)	9,672
Tote	10.02	1.90	119.0476	(1.74)	13,030	10,945	(190)	0	10,755

Returns in 1998	Number of runners	Number of winners	Winning percentage	Total stake (£10 unit) £p	SP returns £p	Profit/(loss) £p	Percentage returned (%)	Tote returns £p	Profit/(loss) £p	Percentage returned (%)
Favourite	143	51	35.7	1,430.00	1,531.97	101.97	107.1	1,507.00	77.00	105.4
Second favourite	137	28.5	20.8	1,370.00	1,483.33	113.33	108.3	1,326.00	(44.00)	96.8
Third favourite	130	8.5	6.6	1,300.00	528.33	(771.67)	40.6	502.00	(798.00)	38.6
Fourth favourite	124	11	8.9	1,240.00	980.00	(260.00)	79.0	1,037.00	(203.00)	83.6
Others - odds up to 14/1	337	19	5.6	3,370.00	2,275.00	(1,095.00)	67.5	2,555.00	(815.00)	75.8
Others - odds 16/1 and higher	495	12	2.4	4,950.00	2,492.00	(2,458.00)	50.3	4,346.00	(604.00)	87.8
All	1,366	130	9.5	13,660.00	9,290.63	(4,369.37)	68.0	11,273.00	(2,387.00)	82.5

	Average number of runners	Average margin per runner (%)	Overall betting margin	(Favourite)/longshot bias (%)	Total stake (£)	Expected return (£)	Effect of Fav/Long bias (£)	Harmonization effect (£)	Actual return (£)
Bookmakers	10.50	2.00	121.0000	(1.75)	13,660	11,289	(198)	(1,800)	9,291
Tote	10.50	1.81	119.0476	(1.75)	13,660	11,474	(201)	0	11,273

Note: Where the number of winners shown includes one-half, this indicates one dead-heat (Gordon Stakes)

Source of data: The Official Form Book (for 1997 and 1998) Raceform

35

Table 2-17 Analysis of betting returns – Newbury

Betting returns based on placing £10 win on every horse that ran (Rule 4 has been applied to starting price returns, where appropriate)

Returns in 1997	Number of runners	Number of winners	Winning percentage	Total stake (£10 unit) £p	SP returns £p	Profit/(loss) £p	Percentage returned (%)	Tote returns £p	Profit/(loss) £p	Percentage returned (%)
Favourite	124	30	24.2	1,240.00	842.33	(397.67)	67.9	788.00	(452.00)	63.5
Second favourite	114	14	12.3	1,140.00	707.50	(432.50)	62.1	612.00	(528.00)	53.7
Third favourite	119	20	16.8	1,190.00	1,420.00	230.00	119.3	1,392.00	202.00	117.0
Fourth favourite	102	10	9.8	1,020.00	910.00	(110.00)	89.2	927.00	(93.00)	90.9
Others - odds up to 14/1	287	23	8.0	2,870.00	2,689.00	(181.00)	93.7	2,945.00	75.00	102.6
Others - odds 16/1 and higher	546	12	2.2	5,460.00	3,110.00	(2,350.00)	57.0	5,471.00	11.00	100.2
All	1,292	109	8.4	12,920.00	9,678.83	(3,241.17)	74.9	12,135.00	(785.00)	93.9

	Average number of runners	Average margin per runner (%)	Overall betting margin	(Favourite/longshot bias %)	Total stake (£)	Expected return (£)	Effect of Fav/Long bias (£)	Harmonization effect (£)	Actual return (£)	Percentage returned (%)
Bookmakers	11.85	2.00	123.7000	11.81	12,920	10,445	1,234	(2,000)	9,679	
Tote	11.85	1.61	119.0476	11.81	12,920	10,853	1,282	0	12,135	

Returns in 1998	Number of runners	Number of winners	Winning percentage	Total stake (£10 unit) £p	SP returns £p	Profit/(loss) £p	Percentage returned (%)	Tote returns £p	Profit/(loss) £p	Percentage returned (%)
Favourite	109	27	24.8	1,090.00	869.64	(220.36)	79.8	786.00	(304.00)	72.1
Second favourite	105	18	17.1	1,050.00	1,000.75	(49.25)	95.3	950.00	(100.00)	90.5
Third favourite	89	15	16.9	890.00	905.00	15.00	101.7	874.00	(16.00)	98.2
Fourth favourite	88	10	11.4	880.00	880.00	0.00	100.0	985.00	105.00	111.9
Others - odds up to 14/1	258	12	4.7	2,580.00	1,365.00	(1,215.00)	52.9	1,524.00	(1,056.00)	59.1
Others - odds 16/1 and higher	422	12	2.8	4,220.00	3,230.00	(990.00)	76.5	5,461.00	1,241.00	129.4
All	1,071	94	8.8	10,710.00	8,250.39	(2,459.61)	77.0	10,580.00	(130.00)	98.8

	Average number of runners	Average margin per runner (%)	Overall betting margin	(Favourite/longshot bias %)	Total stake (£)	Expected return (£)	Effect of Fav/Long bias (£)	Harmonization effect (£)	Actual return (£)	Percentage returned (%)
Bookmakers	11.39	1.94	122.0966	17.61	10,710	8,772	1,545	(2,067)	8,250	
Tote	11.39	1.67	119.0476	17.61	10,710	8,996	1,584	0	10,580	

Source of data: The Official Form Book (for 1997 and 1998)   Raceform

Table 2-18 Analysis of betting returns – Newmarket

Betting returns based on placing £10 win on every horse that ran (Rule 4 has been applied to starting price returns, where appropriate)

Returns in 1997	Number of runners	Number of winners	Winning percentage	Total stake (£10 unit) £p	SP returns £p	Profit/(loss) £p	Percentage returned (%)	Tote returns £p	Profit/loss £p	Percentage returned (%)
Favourite	244	89	36.5	2,440.00	2,611.76	171.76	107.0	2,596.00	156.00	106.4
Second favourite	245	47	19.2	2,450.00	2,394.58	(55.42)	97.7	2,384.00	(66.00)	97.3
Third favourite	233	24	10.3	2,330.00	1,707.50	(622.50)	73.3	1,681.00	(649.00)	72.1
Fourth favourite	227	19	8.4	2,270.00	1,610.00	(660.00)	70.9	1,611.00	(659.00)	71.0
Others - odds up to 14/1	498	25	5.0	4,980.00	2,898.00	(2,082.00)	58.2	3,459.00	(1,521.00)	69.5
Others - odds 16/1 and higher	1,120	22	2.0	11,200.00	5,250.00	(5,950.00)	46.9	9,219.00	(1,981.00)	82.3
All	2,567	226	8.8	25,670.00	16,471.84	(9,198.16)	64.2	20,950.00	(4,720.00)	81.6

	Average number of runners	Average margin per runner (%)	Overall betting margin	(Favourite)/longshot bias (%)	Total stake (£)	Expected return (£)	Effect of Fav/Long bias (£)	Harmonization effect (£)	Actual return (£)
Bookmakers	11.36	2.00	122.7200	(2.84)	25,670	20,918	(594)	(3,852)	16,472
Tote	11.36	1.68	119.0476	(2.84)	25,670	21,563	(613)	0	20,950

Returns in 1998	Number of runners	Number of winners	Winning percentage	Total stake (£10 unit) £p	SP returns £p	Profit/(loss) £p	Percentage returned (%)	Tote returns £p	Profit/loss £p	Percentage returned (%)
Favourite	250	75	30.0	2,500.00	2,237.48	(262.52)	89.5	2,239.00	(261.00)	89.6
Second favourite	244	44	18.0	2,440.00	2,320.83	(119.17)	95.1	2,253.00	(187.00)	92.3
Third favourite	221	18	8.1	2,210.00	1,183.00	(1,027.00)	53.5	1,182.00	(1,028.00)	53.5
Fourth favourite	216	18	8.3	2,160.00	1,465.00	(695.00)	67.8	1,606.00	(554.00)	74.4
Others - odds up to 14/1	596	45	7.6	5,960.00	5,140.00	(820.00)	86.2	6,008.00	48.00	100.8
Others - odds 16/1 and higher	1,181	25	2.1	11,810.00	6,930.50	(4,879.50)	58.7	8,721.00	(3,089.00)	73.8
All	2,708	225	8.3	27,080.00	19,276.81	(7,803.19)	71.2	22,009.00	(5,071.00)	81.3

	Average number of runners	Average margin per runner (%)	Overall betting margin	(Favourite)/longshot bias (%)	Total stake (£)	Expected return (£)	Effect of Fav/Long bias (£)	Harmonization effect (£)	Actual return (£)
Bookmakers	12.04	2.08	125.0432	(3.24)	27,080	21,657	(702)	(1,678)	19,277
Tote	12.04	1.58	119.0476	(3.24)	27,080	22,747	(738)	0	22,009

Source of data: The Official Form Book (for 1997 and 1998) Raceform

Chapter 3
How to use the Market as a Guide

3.1 General principle of 'value'

The word 'value' is used to describe the relationship between the odds being offered, compared with the risks being taken. Expected Value is the 'value' expected from any bet in the long term. The simplest example often used to illustrate this is the spin of the coin. We know that a coin has two sides and assuming it is equally balanced there will be an equal chance it will come down heads or tails. Therefore, if we are going to back 'heads' there is a 0.5 probability that we will be right and a 0.5 probability we will wrong. Along comes a bookmaker, who knows the probabilities, but also wants to make a profit as a reward for offering the service of allowing those who want to bet, to be able to do so. So, the bookmaker offers 4/5 heads and 4/5 tails. As a punter, in the *short term* we might win backing heads or tails as the result will be dependent on how lucky we are. However, in the *long term* we know we will lose as the longer we play the game the more likely it becomes that the actual results will fall in line with the known probabilities.

We can demonstrate this using the following formula:

Expected Value (EV) = Pw x Bw - Pl x Cl, where Pw is the 'probability of winning', Pl is the 'probability of losing', Bw is the 'benefit of winning' and Cl is the 'cost of losing'.

Pw + Pl must always = 1.

So, if we stake £5 on 'heads' the 'cost of losing' would be £5, but if we win we will get back £9, including the return of our stake. Therefore the 'benefit of winning' would be £4.

Therefore, EV = 0.5 x £4 - 0.5 x £5 = £2-£2.50 = -£0.50 (negative).

What this formula is suggesting is that for every £5 bet, in the long term the backer will lose 50p. So, for example, if the punter placed one hundred £5 bets, he would expect to lose £50 overall. The expectation would be that the punter would win £4 fifty times (total £200) and lose £5 fifty times (£250).

As the formula demonstrates, the punter cannot win in the long term as the odds are in the bookmaker's favour, but if the punter knew that the coin was not evenly balanced and accordingly would come down 'heads' 60% of the time, then:

EV = 0.6 x £4 - 0.4 x £5 = £2.40 - 2.00 = £0.40 positive.

Now the punter would expect to win, in the long term, but if the bookmaker found out what the true probabilities were he might change his odds:

1/2 'heads' 5/4 'tails.

Now the revised Expected Value would be, assuming the punter backed 'heads':

EV = 0.6 x £2.50 - 0.4 x £5 = £1.50 - £2.00 = £0.50 (negative)

What this demonstrates is that because bookmakers calculate the odds to allow a margin in their favour, punters can only win if they get the odds wrong. What is meant by getting the odds 'wrong' is that the miscalculation of the true probabilities is greater than the margin taken. For example, calculating the odds on the assumption that a coin was balanced, when it would in fact come down 'heads' 60% of the time would, as illustrated above, be sufficient to give a punter the advantage.

At the time a bet is about to be placed, it is possible to calculate Bw and Cl, but the key is what value we give Pw and Pl. The problem is that these values are subjective and will be based on our own assessment of each race.

One method of assessing Pw and Pl is to convert authoritative ratings such as *Raceform ratings* (as for example published in *Raceform on Saturday*) into probabilities and converting such probabilities into 'minimum acceptable odds'. Where such 'minimum acceptable odds' were below the odds on offer, then 'value' was said to be available. A method of doing this was shown in my book, *The Value Factor in Successful Betting*' (Raceform, 1991).

An argument against setting 'minimum acceptable odds' is that ratings, such as *Raceform ratings*, can only be based on previously known form and that the *'betting market'* may reflect more up-to-date information. For example, it may be that *Raceform's* top rated horse is fancied by his

Table 2-19 Analysis of betting returns - York

Betting returns based on placing £10 win on every horse that ran (Rule 4 has been applied to starting price returns, where appropriate)

Returns in 1997	Number of runners	Number of winners	Winning percentage	Total stake (£10 unit) £p	SP returns £p	Profit/(loss) £p	Percentage returned (%)	Tote returns £p	Profit/(loss) £p	Percentage returned (%)
Favourite	93	27	29.0	930.00	959.46	29.46	103.2	891.00	(39.00)	95.8
Second favourite	106	15.5	14.6	1,060.00	891.83	(168.17)	84.1	901.00	(159.00)	85.0
Third favourite	82	14	17.1	820.00	854.50	34.50	104.2	862.00	42.00	105.1
Fourth favourite	80	8	10.0	800.00	661.00	(139.00)	82.6	710.00	(90.00)	88.8
Others - odds up to 14/1	309	13.5	4.4	3,090.00	1,555.00	(1,535.00)	50.3	1,818.00	(1,272.00)	58.8
Others - odds 16/1 and higher	334	9	2.7	3,340.00	2,040.00	(1,300.00)	61.1	3,348.00	8.00	100.2
All	1,004	87	8.7	10,040.00	6,961.79	(3,078.21)	69.3	8,530.00	(1,510.00)	85.0

	Average number of runners	Average margin per runner (%)	Overall betting margin	(Favourite)/longshot bias (%)	Total stake (£)	Expected return (£)	Effect of Fav/Long bias (£)	Harmonization effect (£)	Actual return (£)
Bookmakers	11.54	2.50	128.8500	1.14	10,040	7,792	89	(919)	6,962
Tote	11.54	1.65	119.0476	1.14	10,040	8,434	96	0	8,530

Returns in 1998	Number of runners	Number of winners	Winning percentage	Total stake (£10 unit) £p	SP returns £p	Profit/(loss) £p	Percentage returned (%)	Tote returns £p	Profit/(loss) £p	Percentage returned (%)
Favourite	111	29	26.1	1,110.00	1,099.18	(10.82)	99.0	1,030.00	(80.00)	92.8
Second favourite	118	17	14.4	1,180.00	810.00	(370.00)	68.6	748.00	(432.00)	63.4
Third favourite	105	15	14.3	1,050.00	1,085.00	35.00	103.3	1,020.00	(30.00)	97.1
Fourth favourite	92	14	15.2	920.00	1,200.00	280.00	130.4	1,393.00	473.00	151.4
Others - odds up to 14/1	357	17	4.8	3,570.00	2,015.00	(1,555.00)	56.4	3,062.00	(508.00)	85.8
Others - odds 16/1 and higher	425	8	1.9	4,250.00	1,950.00	(2,300.00)	45.9	2,912.00	(1,338.00)	68.5
All	1,208	100	8.3	12,080.00	8,159.18	(3,920.82)	67.5	10,165.00	(1,915.00)	84.1

	Average number of runners	Average margin per runner (%)	Overall betting margin	(Favourite)/longshot bias (%)	Total stake (£)	Expected return (£)	Effect of Fav/Long bias (£)	Harmonization effect (£)	Actual return (£)
Bookmakers	12.08	2.33	128.1464	0.18	12,080	9,427	17	(1,285)	8,159
Tote	12.08	1.58	119.0476	0.18	12,080	10,147	18	0	10,165

Note: Where the number of winners shown includes one-half, this indicates one dead-heat (Nunthorpe Stakes)

Source of data: The Official Form Book (for 1997 and 1998) Raceform

connections and as they have backed the animal the odds available are below the 'minimum acceptable'. Market followers will suggest that an even worse scenario is that the odds on offer are greater than the minimum acceptable odds because the connections are *not* backing the horse, knowing it cannot win.

Such views should be taken seriously and one of the objectives of this chapter is to distinguish between market moves resultant from informed opinion and betting adjustments caused by media hype or other reasons that may cause the punter to be wary. What must follow, however, all other things being equal, is that there is a correlation between 'value' and the 'margins' taken by the bookmaker. The lower the margins, the more likely it must be to get 'value', while, conversely, the higher the margins, the less likely it will be to achieve 'value'. Accordingly, the first step in assessing the 'market' is to calculate the betting margin.

3.2 The betting margin

As discussed in the previous chapter, bookmakers 'harmonise' the odds as a method of minimising the risk of losses through insider traders having superior information. This does not, however, mean they are immune from attack and so any attack will affect the market.

Overall, when the harmonisation of odds' effect is taken out, the betting market is a near perfect market as it reaches equilibrium, so that the probabilities, as reflected by the position of each runner in the market, are a fair reflection of what the results will be. In other words, the market manages to absorb the effects of insider trading. However, in doing so the betting margin is affected, and this is why it is necessary to calculate such margin.

Table 3-1 shows how to calculate the betting margin and translate this to a margin per runner. The margin extremes within the 826 races analysed in 1998 were 0.76 per runner at the low end to 7.91 per runner at the other extreme. In this latter case, it can only be assumed that the bookmakers were suffering from a high degree of stress. In the 'Doncaster Exhibition Centre Handicap for 4yo+ rated 0-90 (class C) on June 6 they bet, 6/4, 3/1, 100/30, 7/2 twice, 8/1, 9/1, 10/1, 14/1, 16/1 and 25/1 and when the 6/4 was withdrawn the overall effect was to end up with a margin of 179.1% in a ten-runner race.

The objective of this calculation (which only has to be accurate if the answer is close to a band change) is to place the betting margin (calculated about five minutes before the off) into one of three categories:

Low betting margin ————————————————————————up to 1.50% per runner
Normal (medium and high) betting margin.———————— 1.51% to 2.50% per runner
Very high betting margin ———————————————— 2.51% per runner and higher

In 'low betting margin' races there is a slight bias towards the favourite (as against longshots), so if your selection is not in the first four in the betting a review should be carried out. This bias is probably due to dependable form being associated with better horses and assessment based on form or authoritative ratings should be reliable as there is a low risk of insider trading.

In 'normal' betting margin races, there is a very slight bias towards outsiders, but here the grade of race is important. Grade B and grades E to G races are particularly difficult and it may be worthwhile looking for a horse not in the first four in the betting. There is a favourite bias towards favourites in grade D races and this is particularly evident in grade D maiden races, especially for unraced or little raced two and three year-olds. There is no apparent bias in grade C races.

In 'very high' margin races, there is evidence of insider trading associated with exposed horses. About 80 per cent of these races are won by one of the first four in the betting, compared with about 70 per cent for the remainder. The problem here, though, is that the betting margins are so high that it is impossible for ordinary punters to get anywhere near value and accordingly the recommendation is that races with very high betting margins should be avoided. Compulsive gamblers should head for the Tote and should the resultant Tote dividend be lower than the equivalent returns from the starting price, such compulsive gamblers should conclude that they are so unlucky that it is time to give up.

Before finalising any bet it might be worthwhile remembering that 70 per cent, plus, of all races are won by the first four in the betting (see Table 3-2). As an aid to finding the likely betting position of the winner Table 3-3 (for 1997) and Table 3-4 (for 1998) shows where the winner came from, analyzed by number of runners in each race. If nothing else, what these tables do is to dispel the old racing adage "always back the outsider in races of three runners". As can be seen, out of twenty-two races with three runners, the outsider won only three times, compared to the favourite winning fifteen times.

Knowing that one of the first four in the betting will win 70 per cent plus, of all races, is helpful but if it were possible to eliminate one or two of the first four in the betting, then the advantage would move to the punter. Racing patterns might give a clue as to whether this could be done.

3.3 Racing patterns

A very famous racing personality was once asked if he knew of a winning system. He replied that there was no such thing as a winning system, but the nearest thing to such Utopia was *'to back a good horse until it loses, then back the horse that beats it'*.

This seemed sensible, so the decision was taken to test this on the *trails*. These trails were illustrated in my book, *The Winning Trail* (Raceform 1993). There were five trails:
* The Colts' Classic Trail, starting with the Classic Trial Stakes at Sandown
* The Fillies' Classic Trail, starting with the Musidora Stakes at York
* The Group 1 Trail (for older horses), starting with the Earl of Sefton Stakes at Newmarket
* The Sprint Trail, starting with the Abernant Stakes at Newmarket
* The Stayers' Trail, starting with the Henry II at Sandown.

In each case, the 'first' good horse was deemed to be the winner of the first race in each trail. These are shown as Figures 1 to 7 (covering the five trails in 1997 and 1998) and what is apparent is the rarity of a horse winning consecutive races.

As punters we tend to remember exceptional horses such as Tamarisk and Blue Duster (see Table 3-6) who improved to win three and five consecutive races respectively. More in line with the norm is Top Cees (racing profile follows Table 3-6). Although a very successful horse, Top Cees' wins were spaced apart.

The profile for Top Cees and others that follow can be read as follows:

The first three columns, class, weight and form, denote movement from the previous race.

What normally happens is that the weight goes up as the class of race goes down and vice versa. This means that often the class weight and form symbols are showing variation, so it is impossible to predict what a horse's odds will be in the forthcoming race. However, if all the symbols are = or + the expectation will be that a horse's odds would be higher than in its previous race, while if all the symbols are = or - then the expectation would be that a horse's odds would be lower than in its previous race. Of course, the odds are not absolute as a lot depends on the number of runners in a race, so what we are looking for is the position in the betting, as before:

1. = Favourite
2 = Second favourite
3 = Third favourite
4 = Fourth favourite
5 = Not in the first four in the betting, with odds no greater than 14/1
6 = Odds 16/1 or higher.

If the odds are significantly different to expectations the conclusion is that there has been a market move, but we do not know whether such a market move is the result of informed opinion or ordinary punters speculating. The next step is to ascertain which of these two options apply and whether or not we can take advantage of the situation.

3.4 How to spot insider trading

It is not suggested that punters should change their methods of making selections, but the betting market does provide three levels of confirmation:

Positive Grade A races of up to ten runners, with low betting margins, suggest that the market believes the race will be true in that those with superior public knowledge, such as the availability of *Raceform ratings* will have an advantage.

Neutral Most races, with betting margins no greater than 2.50% per runner, where the betting would appear to be in line with expectations (as, for example, Top Cees' races, other than those shown with a box around the 'Notes' column). In such races, there is no reason why an informed selection based on public information should not be feasible.

Negative All races where the betting margins are greater than 2.50% per runner, or where the odds do not appear in line with expectations. When we are in the negative zone, we need to look for evidence of insider trading.

Insider trading can be found in two types of race:

Two-year-old races where form has not been exposed (horse having first or second race) or where the horse is in a nursery (two-year-old handicap) for the first time, or where the horse races in a higher grade than before.

Older horses, often running in handicaps, who show sudden improvement in form.

In both cases, the first sign is that the odds being offered by the bookmakers are much lower than would be suggested by form. The giveaway is that 'Insider Traders' would (usually) not bet with the Tote, so even allowing for odds' harmonisation, Tote odds will be significantly higher than the returns offered by bookmakers.

To test this, note the position in the betting (1, 2, 3, 4 or 5) and then refer to Table 3-5. If the Tote odds, viewed about five minutes before the off, are outside the upper limit shown in this table then it is possible that bookmakers' odds have been compressed by insider trading. The recommended action is shown as a footnote to this Table 3-5.

It should be noted that the maximum odds, as displayed by the bookmakers, to consider is 12/1. If a 16/1 chance is showing a Tote dividend of (say) £30, then it is likely that what is being witnessed is nothing more than the effect of bookmakers' odds harmonisation.

Examples of perceived 'insider trading' as suggested by market variations are shown under the headings "Talking two-year-olds" and 'Seasoned racers'.

3.5 Where to bet

Taking everything in account and with the selection made, the only decision left is whether to bet with the bookmakers or with the Tote. For racegoers, this decision will be made easier through displays on bookmakers' boards and Tote screens, but those betting in a betting shop may not have this information to hand. In any event, Tote odds can change significantly in the final three minutes before the off. So a key question for a punter in every race is: Which betting medium is going to pay the better return, the starting price or the Tote?

A key factor relative to this decision is the number of runners in the race. Bookmakers' margins increase as the number of runners go up, but the Tote makes a fixed deduction from each race. In the case of the win pool this deduction is currently 16% and has been this figure for a number of years.

Bookmakers' margins can be calculated on the basis of working out how much money would have to be placed on each horse to return £100. So, for example, 3/1 would be £25, 4/1 would be £20, 9/1 would be £10 and so on. The total is then expressed as a percentage, as shown in the Official Form Book. If the required amount to guarantee a return of £100 was £120, then the official Form Book would show the betting margin of 120.0%. This would be the equivalent of a 16.67% deduction from the total stakes. Accordingly, as the Tote deduct 16.0% from their win pool their betting margin on each race is 119.0% (119.047619% to be exact).

In 1998, the average bookmakers' margin for the seven racecourses tested was 2.07% per runner, so for a nine runner race the average margin would be 118.6% and for a ten runner race it would be 120.7%. Therefore, all things being equal, we would expect bookmakers' returns to beat Tote returns in races with two to nine runners, and Tote returns to beat bookmakers' returns in races of ten or more runners. Over the long term, this is what happens, as a review of Tables 3-3 and 3-4 indicates. Overall, bookmakers beat the Tote in races with up to eight runners, they were virtually the same when there were nine runners (although the Tote marginally came out on top) and the Tote beat the bookmakers by a fair margin in races with ten or more runners.

However, things are not equal and the prime reason for this is the fact that bookmakers 'harmonize' their odds. Therefore, what tends to happen is that bookmakers beat the Tote if the first or second favourite wins, it is very close between the two if the third (bookmakers have a slight edge) or fourth favourite (Tote has a slight edge) wins and the Tote beat the bookmakers by a fair margin if the fifth favourite (not first to fourth favourite with odds up to 14/1) wins and by a large margin if an outsider (odds 16/1 or greater) wins. However, betting patterns are further compli-cated by changes according to grade of race, overall bookmakers' betting margins and whether or not a particular race has been the subject of insider trading. All these factors have been incorpo-rated into Table 3-9 which is provided primarily for betting shop punters to assist in the decision as to which betting medium to choose. Tables 3-7 and 3-8 show actual comparative returns for the seven racecourses in 1997 and 1998.

Chapter 4
Market 'form'

Market intelligence conducted by the bookmakers seems to be very effective, as many highly-rated horses at the end of the season start their careers being sent off favourite for their first race. If they do well, they might be put up in class in their next race and the expectation would be that in most cases their market position in the betting would reflect this. A victory in the conditions race following the maiden, might result in an attempt at a grade A race and the subsequent odds are likely to reflect the difficulty of the task.

Horses not improving so much might be put into handicap company as quickly as possible and here the odds will reflect the quality of the race, relative to past form. The difficulty is always assessing the quality of the race with the weight being carried.

If the odds on offer about a particular horse appears to be slightly low (as against being mean-ingfully depressed) then the reason may well be because the trainer is known to have good hors-es and is highly regarded. In other cases, low odds could possibly indicate that a particular horse was being backed by those with inside information. Long odds could mean the opposite, that for whatever reason, success was not expected in the race in question. The difficulty for the ordinary punter is trying to ascertain what is going on and seeing if the betting market can yield any clues. For example, a punter might have selected a horse that is a long price and wonder if the 'stable' would let any of their winners go off at odds in double figures. In other words, does the market truly reflect the probability of success?

As discussed in earlier chapters, where insiders are backing one of the favourites in the race, the betting margin will tend to go out, but ordinary punters will not be able to work out from the mar-ket which horse is the subject of such special attention. On the other hand, where improving hors-es, at the time not one of the favourites, are being backed, it may well be possible to deduce what is going on, but such occurrences are relatively rare.

As an aid to assessing the betting market, this chapter shows the 'market' form for over five hundred horses. To be selected, each horse had to have a Raceform rating of 90 or more at the end of the 1998 season, and had to have won at least one turf race in that year in Great Britain. 'Market' form shows the Raceform rating, the name of the trainer as shown in the Form Book, the number of runs and wins in the season, and the position in the betting each time the horse won. The mean of the betting position, when races were won, is shown as 'Average winning rating'. Foreign races, where the Form Book did not include details of the betting, are excluded, as are all All-Weather races. 'Position in the betting when winning numbers' are as follows:

0 = Favourite and odds-on.
1 = Favourite, but odds against.
2 = Second favourite, or joint second favourite, or co-second favourite
3 = No more than two horses with shorter odds in the race, but can be joint or co-third favourites.
4 = No more than three horses with shorter odds in the race, but can be joint or co-fourth favourites.
5 = No more than four horses with shorter odds in the race and odds no greater than 14/1.
6 = Odds 16/1 or higher.

Table 3-1 Calculation of betting margin (quick method)

Step 1 Make a note of the odds of each horse, putting into groups where appropriate, and add up the values.
Step 2 Deduct 100 from the addition in step 1.
Step 3 Divide the answer in step 2, by the number of runners.

Note that complete accuracy is only required if answer is close to a band change. The four bands are given below.

Bands: Low margin - up to 1.50% per runner. Medium margin - 1.51% to 2.00% per runner. High margin - 2.01% to 2.50% per runner.
Very high margin - 2.51% and above per runner.

Value Odds on	Odds
	1/1
52	11/10
55	6/5
56	5/4
58	11/8
60	6/4
62	13/8
64	7/4
65	15/8
67	2/1
68	85/40
69	9/4
71	5/2
73	11/4
75	3/1
77	100/30
78	7/2
80	4/1
82	9/2
83	5/1
85	11/2
86	6/1
87	13/2
87	7/1
88	15/2
89	8/1
89	17/2
90	9/1
91	10/1
92	11/1
92	12/1
93	13/1
93	14/1
94	15/1
94	16/1
95	20/1
96	22/1
96	25/1
97	28/1
97	33/1
97	35/1
98	40/1
98	50/1
99	66/1
99	75/1
99	100/1

Value				
One horse	Two horses	Three horses	Four horses	Five horses
50				
48	95			
45	91			
44	88			
42	84			
40	80			
38	76			
36	73			
35	70			
33	67			
32	64	96		
31	62	92		
29	57	86		
27	53	80		
25	50	75		
23	46	69	92	
22	44	67	89	
20	40	60	80	
18	36	55	73	91
17	33	50	67	83
15	31	46	62	77
14	29	43	57	71
13	27	40	53	67
13	25	38	50	63
12	24	35	47	59
11	22	33	44	56
11	21	32	42	53
10	20	30	40	50
9	18	27	36	45
8	17	25	33	42
8	15	23	31	38
7	14	21	29	36
7	13	20	27	33
6	13	19	25	31
6	12	18	24	29
5	10	14	19	24
4	9	13	17	22
4	8	12	15	19
3	7	10	14	17
3	6	9	12	15
3	6	8	11	14
2	5	7	10	12
2	4	6	8	10
1	3	4	6	7
1	3	4	5	7
1	2	3	4	5

Example of calculation: Odds 4/1, 11/2, 6/1, 7/1, 15/2, 9/1 twice, 14/1 four times = 20+15+14+13+12+20+27 = 121 - 100 = 21, divided by 11 = 1.91
The answer of 1.91 would be classified as a 'medium' margin.

Table 3-2   Cumulative percentages of winning favourites

Percentage of total		Favourite	Favourite + second favourite	First, second and third favourites	First, second, third and fourth fav.
	1997				
10.2	Ascot	22.6	42.9	50.0	64.3
16.0	Doncaster	27.3	49.2	60.6	72.0
7.2	Epsom	37.3	55.9	76.3	81.4
15.7	Goodwood	37.7	53.8	66.2	75.4
13.1	Newbury	27.5	40.4	58.7	67.9
27.3	Newmarket	39.4	60.2	70.8	79.2
10.5	York	31.0	48.9	64.9	74.1
100.0	Seven racecourses	32.9	51.6	64.5	74.1
20.0	Grade A races	35.2	59.7	70.6	78.5
14.4	Grade B races	28.6	40.3	54.6	63.9
23.1	Grade C races	30.9	50.8	62.8	73.3
32.5	Grade D races	37.9	54.6	68.0	77.0
10.0	Grade E to G races	22.9	43.4	59.0	72.3
20.0	Low margin races (up to 1.50% per runner)	31.5	50.3	61.2	72.1
39.1	Medium margin races (1.51% to 2.00% per runner)	32.2	49.4	60.5	72.6
23.4	High margin races (2.01% to 2.50% per runner)	33.0	51.0	67.5	73.2
17.5	Very high margin races (2.51% + per runner)	35.9	58.6	73.1	80.7

Percentage of total		Favourite	Favourite + second favourite	First, second and third favourites	First, second, third and fourth fav.
	1998				
10.2	Ascot	26.2	48.8	60.7	73.8
16.4	Doncaster	35.6	51.9	60.0	68.9
7.0	Epsom	24.1	48.3	56.9	67.2
15.7	Goodwood	39.2	61.2	67.7	76.2
11.4	Newbury	28.7	47.9	63.8	74.5
27.2	Newmarket	33.3	52.9	60.9	68.9
12.1	York	29.0	46.0	61.0	75.0
100.0	Seven racecourses	32.2	51.9	61.9	71.8
20.6	Grade A races	32.9	55.6	68.8	77.1
15.5	Grade B races	25.8	44.5	50.8	61.7
21.4	Grade C races	28.8	45.2	57.1	72.3
31.8	Grade D races	39.2	59.3	67.7	74.5
10.7	Grade E to G races	26.1	46.6	56.8	67.0
16.5	Low margin races (up to 1.50% per runner)	34.6	51.8	61.8	70.6
34.6	Medium margin races (1.51% to 2.00% per runner)	27.6	46.9	57.3	68.2
29.9	High margin races (2.01% to 2.50% per runner)	31.6	50.2	61.1	71.7
19.0	Very high margin races (2.51% + per runner)	39.5	63.7	71.3	79.6

How to read this table: The percentages indicate the overall percentage of winners that would have been backed had the punter backed every favourite, favourite and second favourite etc. The percentages are based on the inclusion of joint and co favourites, where appropriate

45

Table 3-3 Analysis of betting returns by Number of Runners per race

Seven racecourses - 1997 (Ascot, Doncaster, Epsom, Goodwood, Newbury, Newmarket and York)

Number of runners per race	Total number of winners	Favourite	Second favourite	Third favourite	Fourth favourite	Others odds to 14/1	Others odds 16/1 and higher	Starting price payments to £10 stake £p	SP % of stake returned %	Tote dividends to £10 stake £p	Tote divs % of stake returned %
2	2	1	1					32.22	80.6	30.00	75.0
3	10	5	3	2				280.31	93.4	243.00	81.0
4	29	17	8	3	1			870.48	75.0	761.00	65.6
5	54	26	9	10	3	6		2,350.38	87.1	2,173.00	80.5
6	66	26	17	8	5	8	2	3,592.25	90.7	3,359.00	84.8
7	69	24	10	10	8	11	6	4,239.93	87.8	4,220.00	87.4
8	79	25	22	6	7	15	4	5,020.34	79.4	5,212.00	82.5
9	68	23	13	10	5	12	5	5,283.23	86.3	5,676.00	92.7
10	67	22	10	7	6	13	9	5,309.90	79.3	5,613.00	83.8
11	56	17	8	11	10	8	2	4,012.35	65.1	4,290.00	69.6
12	55	22	9	7	4	10	3	4,031.10	61.1	5,279.00	80.0
13	40	13	5	5	5	6	6	3,717.36	71.5	4,423.00	85.1
14	37	10	9	4	3	10	1	2,906.25	56.1	3,014.00	58.2
15	33	8	6.5	6	3	6.5	3	2,950.27	59.6	3,754.00	75.8
16	26	9	7	3	1	6	0	1,988.32	47.8	2,306.00	55.4
17	11	1	2	2	1	2	3	1,420.00	75.9	1,721.00	92.0
18	24	4	1	5	5	2	7	3,262.50	75.5	4,024.00	93.1
19	18	3	2	3	2	5	3	2,270.00	66.4	3,096.00	90.5
20	17	3	2	1	1	3	7	2,738.00	80.5	4,940.00	145.3
21	11	3	1	1	2	2	2	1,367.50	59.2	2,082.00	90.1
22	20	3	2	1	2	3	9	3,085.00	70.1	4,983.00	113.3
23	8	2	2	0	3	0	1	815.00	44.3	934.00	50.8
24	5	1	0	1	1	1	1	595.00	49.6	985.00	82.1
25	5	0	2	0	0	1	2	830.00	66.4	1,081.00	86.5
26	1	0	0	0	1	0	0	100.00	38.5	101.00	38.8
27	0	0	0	0	0	0	0	0.00	0.0	0.00	0.0
28	4	0	2	0	0	0	2	725.00	64.7	834.00	74.5
29	5	1	1	1	0	0	2	682.50	47.1	1,678.00	115.7
30	4	2	0	0	0	0	2	570.00	47.5	709.00	59.1
31	1	0	0	0	0	0	1	170.00	54.8	184.00	59.4
32	1	0	0	0	0	0	1	170.00	53.1	261.00	81.6
36	1	1	0	0	0	0	0	50.00	13.9	58.00	16.1
	827	272	154.5	107	79	130.5	84	65,435.19	70.1	78,024.00	83.5

46

Table 3-4 Analysis of betting returns by Number of Runners per race

Seven racecourses - 1998 (Ascot, Doncaster, Epsom, Goodwood, Newbury, Newmarket and York)

Number of runners per race	Total number of winners	Favourite	Second favourite	Third favourite	Fourth favourite	Others odds to 14/1	Others odds 16/1 and higher	Starting price payments to £10 stake £p	SP % of stake returned %	Tote dividends to £10 stake £p	Tote divs % of stake returned %
2	3	1	2					67.75	112.9	64.00	106.7
3	12	10	1	1				228.52	63.5	219.00	60.8
4	34	18	11	1	4			1,176.82	86.5	1,028.00	75.6
5	46	22	12	7	4	0	1	1,926.24	83.7	1,797.00	78.1
6	70	37	14.5	5.5	5	7	1	3,288.42	78.3	2,899.00	69.0
7	72	22	19	7	7	10	7	5,113.25	101.5	5,002.00	99.2
8	69	16	10	16	11	13	3	4,692.45	85.0	4,731.00	85.7
9	63	30	12	2	3	11	5	4,301.00	75.9	4,398.00	77.6
10	62	18	13	8	6	10	7	4,708.77	75.9	5,296.00	85.4
11	54	15	7	8	7	14	3	4,419.73	74.4	5,174.00	87.1
12	41	8	10	6	6	9	2	3,290.34	66.9	3,721.00	75.6
13	34	7	5	3	5	11	3	3,198.75	72.4	3,956.00	89.5
14	30	7	7	3	2	5	6	3,090.50	73.6	4,263.00	101.5
15	38	9	7	4	3	6	9	4,878.00	85.6	6,180.00	108.4
16	44	10	13	3	4	11	3	4,000.41	56.8	4,613.00	65.5
17	24	11	4	2	3	2	2	1,787.21	43.8	2,470.00	60.5
18	13	3	1	1	1	4	3	1,430.00	61.1	1,806.00	77.2
19	16	4	2	0	3	1	5	1,706.58	56.1	2,737.00	90.0
20	23	3	4	1	4	6	6	3,080.00	67.0	3,722.00	80.9
21	16	4	0	1	1	3	7	2,592.00	77.1	4,390.00	130.7
22	19	3	2	0	0	6	7	3,060.00	73.2	4,140.00	99.0
23	8	3	1	1	0	2	2	848.25	46.1	1,164.00	63.3
24	9	1	0	0	2	2	3	1,440.00	66.7	2,288.00	105.9
25	4	0	1	0	1	2	0	470.00	47.0	534.00	53.4
26	5	1	0	0	0	0	2	730.00	56.2	1,155.00	88.8
27	2	1	0	0	0	0	0	368.75	68.3	497.00	92.0
28	3	0	2	0	0	3	1	410.00	48.8	693.00	82.5
29	7	1	1	0	0	0	2	905.00	44.6	1,000.00	49.3
30	2	1	0	1	0	0	0	150.00	25.0	161.00	26.8
31	1	0	1	0	0	0	0	90.00	29.0	55.00	17.7
32	1	0	0	0	0	0	0	210.00	65.6	201.00	62.8
35	1	0	0	0	0	0	1	210.00	60.0	277.00	79.1
	826	266	162.5	82.5	82	140	93	67,868.74	70.8	80,631.00	84.1

Figure 1   **The Colts' Classic Trail**

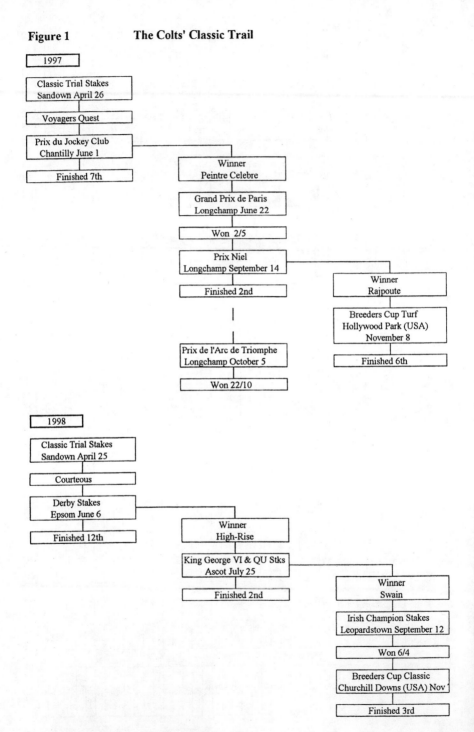

48

Figure 2   **The Fillies' Classic Trail**

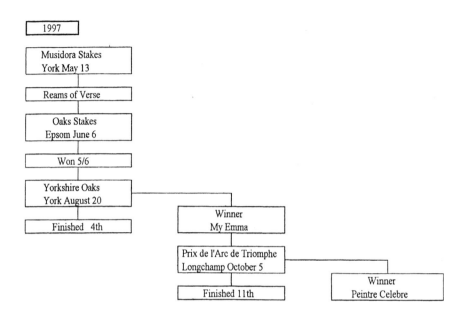

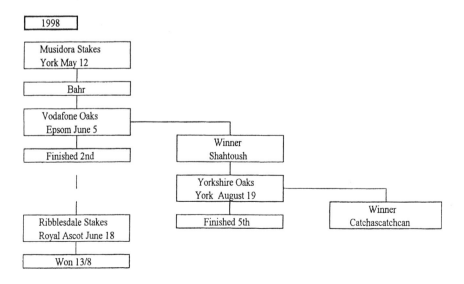

Figure 3   The Group 1 Trail 1997

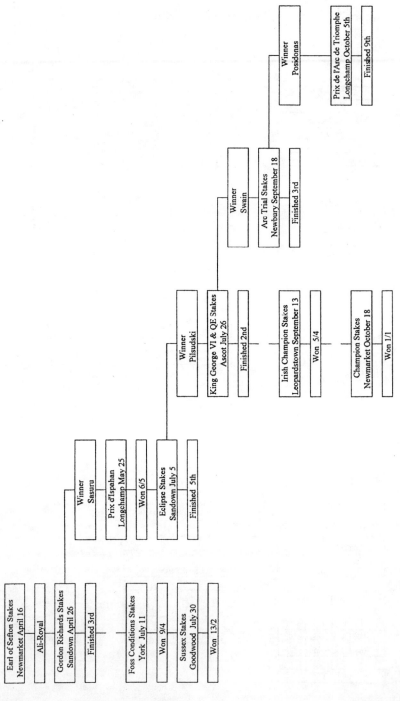

Earl of Sefton Stakes Newmarket April 16	Ali-Royal
	Finished 3rd

Gordon Richards Stakes Sandown April 26

Winner Sasuru

Prix d'Ispahan Longchamp May 25 — Won 6/5

Eclipse Stakes Sandown July 5 — Finished 5th

Foss Conditions Stakes York July 11 — Won 9/4

Sussex Stakes Goodwood July 30 — Won 13/2

Winner Pilsudski

King George VI & QE Stakes Ascot July 26 — Finished 2nd

Irish Champion Stakes Leopardstown September 13 — Won 5/4

Champion Stakes Newmarket October 18 — Won 1/1

Winner Swain

Arc Trial Stakes Newbury September 18 — Finished 3rd

Winner Posidonas

Prix de l'Arc de Triomphe Longchamp October 5th — Finished 9th

Figure 4   **The Group 1 Trail 1998**

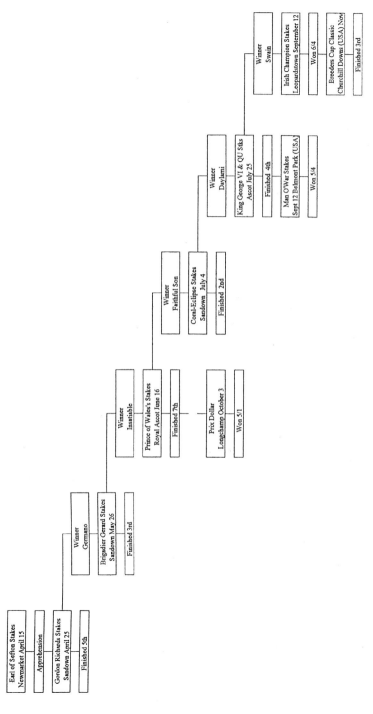

Earl of Sefton Stakes
Newmarket April 15

Apprehension

Gordon Richards Stakes
Sandown April 25

Finished 5th

Winner
Germano

Brigadier Gerard Stakes
Sandown May 26

Finished 3rd

Winner
Instabile

Prince of Wales's Stakes
Royal Ascot June 16

Finished 7th

Prix Dollar
Longchamp October 3

Won 5/1

Winner
Faithful Son

Coral-Eclipse Stakes
Sandown July 4

Finished 2nd

Winner
Daylami

King George VI & QU Stks
Ascot July 25

Finished 4th

Man O'War Stakes
Sept 12 Belmont Park (USA)

Won 5/4

Winner
Swain

Irish Champion Stakes
Leopardstown September 12

Won 6/4

Breeders Cup Classic
Churchill Downs (USA) Nov

Finished 3rd

51

Figure 5   **The Sprint Trail 1997**

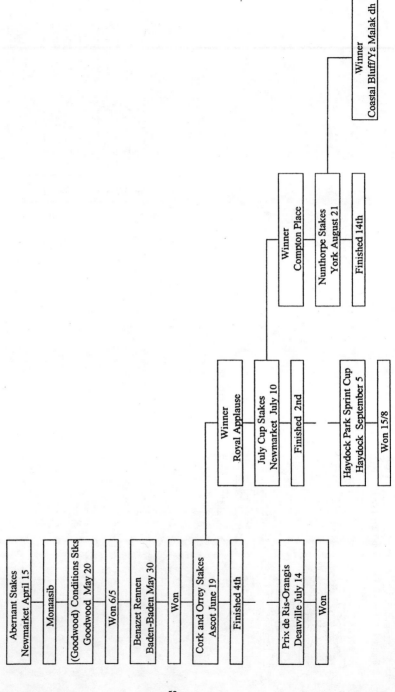

Figure 6   The Sprint Trail 1998

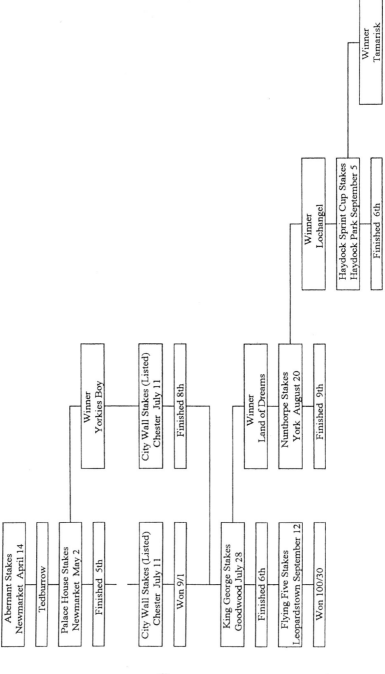

Abernant Stakes
Newmarket April 14

Tedburrow

Palace House Stakes
Newmarket May 2

Finished 5th

Winner
Yorkies Boy

City Wall Stakes (Listed)
Chester July 11

Won 9/1

City Wall Stakes (Listed)
Chester July 11

Finished 8th

King George Stakes
Goodwood July 28

Finished 6th

Winner
Land of Dreams

Nunthorpe Stakes
York August 20

Finished 9th

Flying Five Stakes
Leopardstown September 12

Won 100/30

Winner
Lochangel

Haydock Sprint Cup Stakes
Haydock Park September 5

Finished 6th

Winner
Tamarisk

53

Figure 7   The Stayers' Trail

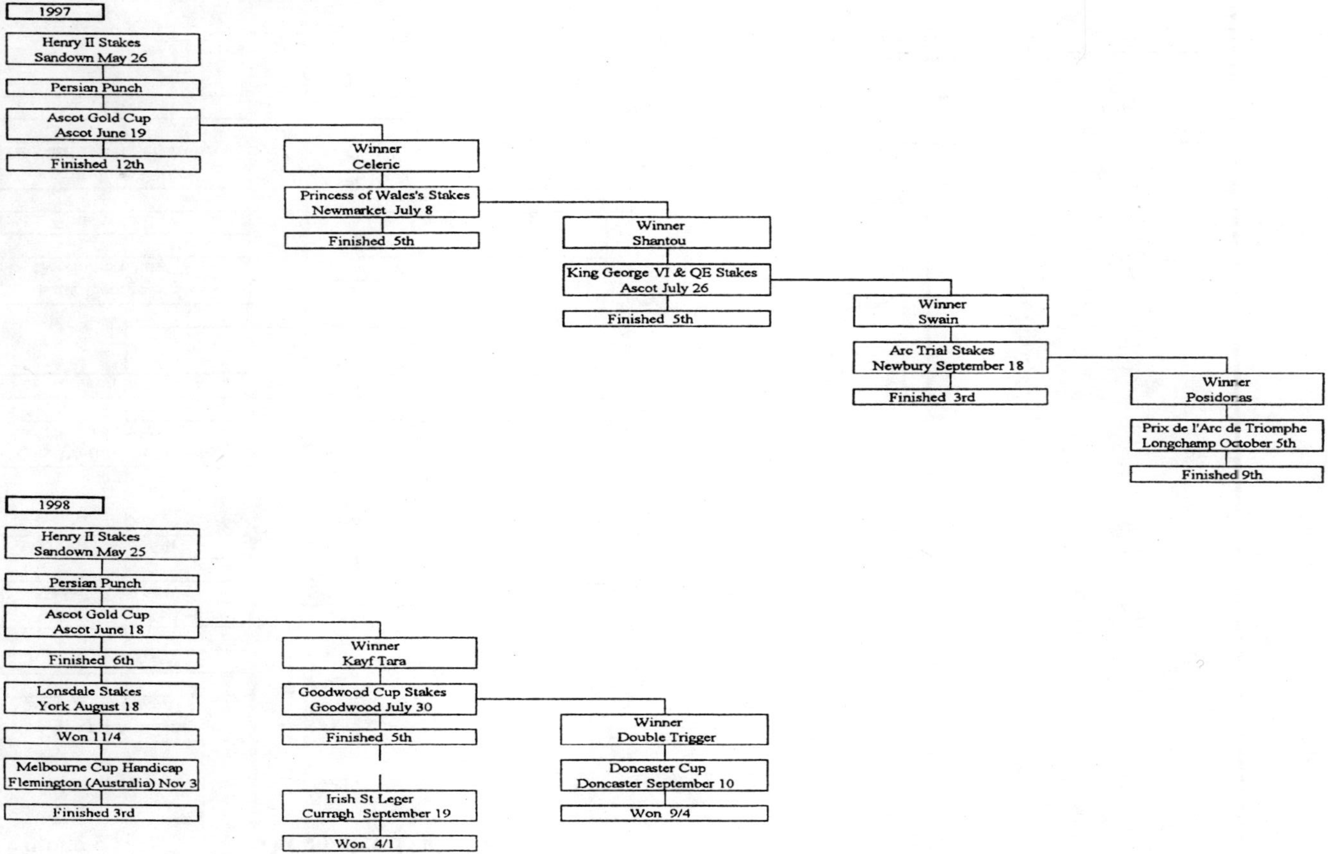

1997

Henry II Stakes
Sandown May 26

Persian Punch

Ascot Gold Cup
Ascot June 19

Finished 12th

Winner
Celeric

Princess of Wales's Stakes
Newmarket July 8

Finished 5th

Winner
Shantou

King George VI & QE Stakes
Ascot July 26

Finished 5th

Winner
Swain

Arc Trial Stakes
Newbury September 18

Finished 3rd

Winner
Posidoras

Prix de l'Arc de Triomphe
Longchamp October 5th

Finished 9th

1998

Henry II Stakes
Sandown May 25

Persian Punch

Ascot Gold Cup
Ascot June 18

Finished 6th

Lonsdale Stakes
York August 18

Won 11/4

Melbourne Cup Handicap
Flemington (Australia) Nov 3

Finished 3rd

Winner
Kayf Tara

Goodwood Cup Stakes
Goodwood July 30

Finished 5th

Irish St Leger
Curragh September 19

Won 4/1

Winner
Double Trigger

Doncaster Cup
Doncaster September 10

Won 9/4

54

Table 3-5 Expected Tote dividend range for Starting Prices with position in betting

All Tote dividends shown are to £1 stake, with the return of the winning stake included

Position in betting — Starting price/ odds near to start of race	Favourite or Second fav. Tote minimum dividend £p	Favourite or Second fav. Tote maximum dividend £p	Third/fourth favourite Tote minimum dividend £p	Third/fourth favourite Tote maximum dividend £p	Fifth favourite Tote minimum dividend £p	Fifth favourite Tote maximum dividend £p
1/5 to 1/2	1.20	1.70				
8/15 to 1/1	1.40	2.20				
11/10 to 11/8	1.70	2.50				
6/4 to 15/8	1.90	3.20				
2/1	2.20	3.30				
9/4	2.50	3.70				
5/2	2.80	3.90				
11/4	2.90	4.10				
3/1 to 7/2	3.00	5.40	3.20	5.60		
4/1	3.40	6.00	3.60	6.20		
9/2	4.00	6.70	4.20	6.90	4.50	7.20
5/1	4.30	7.20	4.50	7.40	5.60	8.50
11/2	4.70	7.80	4.90	8.00	6.00	9.00
6/1	5.00	8.00	5.20	8.90	6.30	9.50
13/2	5.60	8.50	5.80	9.00	6.70	10.00
7/1	6.00	9.20	6.20	9.40	6.80	11.00
15/2	6.70	10.30	7.00	11.00	7.10	11.50
8/1	7.50	11.50	8.00	11.80	7.20	12.00
9/1	8.00	12.50	8.20	14.00	8.40	14.40
10/1	8.40	13.00	8.70	14.50	9.50	15.00
11/1			10.10	15.00	11.00	15.60
12/1					11.50	20.00

Note: Tote dividends should be in the range shown in this table. If Tote divdends are showing HIGHER than the figure in the appropriate 'maximum' column, then it is possible that 'insider trading' has compressed bookmakers' odds and it may be beneficial to back the affected horse on the Tote. If, on the other hand, the Tote dividends are showing LOWER than the figure in the MINIMUM column, then a bet with the bookmakers may be worthwhile.

Remember, however, the market is not always right and there can be no guarantee of success.

Table 3-6

	Down - Up + Same =	Down - Up + Same =*	Better - Worse + Same =	Down - Up + ##
## blank = no decision (* =) = within 3lb.				

TOP CEES

Class	Weight	Form	Decision	Race number	Date	Racecourse
				1	8/4/93	Leicester
=	=			2	24/4/93	Salisbury
+	=		-	3	22/5/93	Lingfield
-	+	=		4	25/6/93	Newmarket
+	-	=		5	9/7/93	York
=	+		-	6	28/7/93	Goodwood
=/-	+	+	+	7	10/6/94	York
-	+	-		8	16/7/94	Newbury
=/+	-	+		9	9/9/94	Doncaster
-	=	=	-	10	24/9/94	Haydock
=	-	=		11	7/10/94	Ascot
-	=	+		12	23/3/95	Doncaster
+	-	=		13	18/4/95	Newmarket
+	=	=		14	10/5/95	Chester
-	+	-		15	20/6/95	Ascot
+	=	+	+	16	6/9/95	Doncaster
=	-	=		17	14/10/95	Newmarket
-	+	-		18	6/7/96	Sandown
=	=	+		19	20/7/96	Newmarket
+	-	-		20	4/8/96	Chester
+	-	+		21	21/8/96	York
-	+	=		22	18/4/97	Newbury
+	-	-		23	7/5/97	Chester
=	+	-		24	28/6/97	Newcastle
=	=	+		25	29/7/97	Goodwood
=	-	=		26	20/8/97	York
-	+	=		27	20/9/97	Ayr
+	-	-		28	18/10/97	Newmarket
-	+	=		29	15/4/98	Newmarket
+	-	-		30	6/5/98	Chester
=	-	+		31	12/6/98	York
-	+	-		32	20/6/98	Ayr
+	-	-		33	2/8/98	Chester
=/+	+	=/+	+	34	17/8/98	Pontefract

Comment: Top Cees hit the headlines on April 18 1995 when, starting 5/1 favourite at Newmarket, he got himself boxed in and finished fifth, beaten two and a half lengths. For some reason, the 'media' went mad and his trainer, Mrs L. Ramsden and her jockey, K. Fallon, were effectively accused of cheating. Some said that they would not dare to allow the horse to win his next race, the Chester Cup, and punters, misled into believing such a theory, allowed the horse to be sent off at 8/1, and were understandably silenced when Top Cees won the race in a canter. Events got completely out of control and were only concluded with the Ramsdens winning a libel action. Had there been a rational debate at the time of the Chester Cup, it would not have been difficult, admittedly in hindsight, to work out what had happened. In the previous season, at Haydock on September 24, when trained by P. Harris, the Raceform race reader had commented: "Top Cees was

56

Race grade	Race type	Weight	Finishing position	Number of runners	Starting price	SP position	Notes
D	Maiden	9-0	10	18	20/1	6	
D	Maiden	9-0	1	14	33/1	6	
C	H'cap 0-100	9-1	2	13	11/1	5	Win improves SP position
C	H'cap 0-95	9-7	2	6	3/1	1	Price too short
B	H'cap 0-105	8-7	2	5	4/1	4	Position expected
B	H'cap 0-105	9-1	12	16	33/1	6	Price too high. Why?
B	H'cap 0-95	9-7	5	10	10/1	5	Confirms previous comment
C	H'cap 0-90	10-0	6	8	9/1	5	
C	H'cap 0-100	9-9	7	16	12/1	5	
C	H'cap 0-90	9-8	4	11	9/1	5	Positioning should be lower
C	H'cap 0-90	9-2	10	13	10/1	5	
E	H'cap 0-80	9-0	6	23	9/1	4	
C	H'cap 0-90	8-9	5	16	5/1	1	Favouritism (due to media attention) not justified
B	Handicap	8-8	1	18	8/1	4	Position expected
C	H'cap 0-90	9-6	19	27	10/1	3	
B	H'cap 0-105	9-6	4	6	13/2	4	SP position + confirmed
B	Handicap	8-11	3	21	4/1	1	
D	H'cap 0-85	10-0	7	13	11/1	5	
D	H'cap 0-85	9-12	1	8	6/1	4	·
C	H'cap 0-95	8-13	7	9	13/8	1	Price too short (over-reaction to form)
B	Handicap	8-1	6	21	16/1	6	SP position as expected
C	H'cap 0-100	9-8	2	12	11/1	5	
B	Handicap	8-11	1	12	11/2	3	
B	Handicap	9-7	5	18	5/2	1	Price too short (over-reaction to form)
B	H'cap 0-105	9-4	5	13	9/1	5	SP position as expected
B	Handicap	8-10	6	21	16/1	6	
C	H'cap 0-90	10-0	1	13	9/2	1	Price too short - Tote £4.40
B	Handicap	8-12	2	31	5/1	1	Price expected due to form
C	4yo+ Handicap (0-95)	9-11	3	21	9/1	2	
B	Handicap	9-7	13	18	11/2	1	Price based on previous victories in Chester Cup
B	H'cap 0-100	9-2	2	9	11/2	3	
C	H'cap 0-95	10-0	1	4	11/10	1	
B	H'cap 0-100	9-0	2	4	13.8	1	
B	H'cap 0-105	9-10	1	7	9/2	4	SP position outwards confirmed

beginning to stay on when denied a clear run over two furlongs out. He finds this trip too sharp" (10f 120y). It was known therefore, that Top Cees did, on occasions, get himself into trouble, and that he wanted longer distances. It was not denied at the libel case that J. Ramsden, husband of the trainer, had the occasional bet and no doubt he had superior information to ordinary punters, but the racing profile of Top Cees does not provide any evidence of "insider trading". One of thirty-four races, there were only two occasions when the odds on offer looked particularly low, but in both cases the betting margins were not abnormal, and the Tote dividend was in the expected range.

Table 3-6 Examples of 'normal' racing profiles (continued)

TAMARISK

	Down -	Down -	Better -	Down -
	Up +	Up +	Worse +	Up +
	Same =	Same =	Same =	Same = ##

blank = no decision
(* =) = within 3lb.

Race number	Date	Racecourse	Race grade	Race type	Weight	Finishing position	Number of runners	Starting price	SP position	Notes
1	2/8/97	Goodwood	D	Maiden (unraced 2yo)	9-0	1	9	11/4	1	
2	10/9/97	Kempton	C	2yo c & g conditions	9-1	1	11	10/11	1	
3	30/10/97	Newmarket	B	2yo conditions	9-0	1	13	5/4	1	
4	18/10/97	Newmarket	A	2yo c & f Group 1	9-0	2	7	9/2	3	Market indicates no bet
5	2/5/98	Newmarket	A	3yo classic	9-0	16	18	28/1	6	2000 Guineas form ignored
6	30/5/98	Lingfield	A	3yo + Listed	8-6	1	7	9/4	1	
7	9/5/98	Newmarket	A	3yo+ Group 1	8-13	2	17	5/1	2	Value, on form
8	5/9/98	Haydock	A	3yo+ Group 1	8-12	1	13	13/2	4	

Class	Weight	Form	Decision
+	=	-	=
+	=	=	=
+	=	=	=
=	=	=	+
-	-	+	+
-	+	-	=
=	=	=	=

BLUE DUSTER

	Down -	Down -	Better -	Down -
	Up +	Up +	Worse +	Up +
	Same =	Same =	Same =	Same = ##

blank = no decision
(* =) = within 3lb.

Race number	Date	Racecourse	Race grade	Race type	Weight	Finishing position	Number of runners	Starting price	SP position	Notes
1	29/5/95	Sandown	D	2yo f maiden	8-11	1	9	8/11	1	
2	21/6/95	(Royal) Ascot	A	2yo f Group 3	8-8	1	12	7/4	1	
3	22/7/95	Ascot	A	2yo f Group 3	9-0	1	7	30/100	1	
4	26/9/95	Newmarket	A	2yo f Group 1	8-11	1	5	4/5	1	
5	21/7/96	Yarmouth	C	3yo f conditions	9-2	1	5	4/5	1	Reported not to have grown
6	11/8/96	Deauville	A(e)	3yo+ Group 1	8-8	5	9	not known	nk	
7	7/9/96	Haydock	A	3yo+ Group 1	8-9	2	11	9/1	5	Price due to comment and form
8	15/5/97	York	A	3yo+ Group 3	8-11	3	10	100/30	2	
9	19/6/97	(Royal) Ascot	A	3yo+ Group 3	8-10	7	23	13/2	2	

Class	Weight	Form	Decision
+	+	-	=
=	+	=	=
+	=	=	=
-	+	=	=
=	-	=	+
=	=	+	=
-	=	-	-
=	=	=	=

Table 3-7   Analysis of betting returns 1997

	Percentage of stake returned										
	Favourite		Second favourite		Third favourite		Fourth favourite		Odds to 14/1 (SP)		Odds 16/1+ (SP)	
	SP	Tote	SP	Tote	SP	Tote	SP	Tote	SP	Tote	SP	Tote
Ascot - all races	77.1	64.9	104.0	94.0	57.9	50.4	121.4	116.5	73.4	85.4	82.6	96.7
Up to 5 runners	134.4	120.0	71.9	63.8	45.0	47.0	0.0	0.0	240.0	134.0	0.0	0.0
6-10 runners	74.9	61.0	77.6	70.3	51.5	43.0	93.8	88.0	130.5	136.4	155.6	127.1
11-15 runners	75.0	64.6	146.7	138.3	85.0	72.0	243.2	233.6	33.7	40.8	35.8	40.6
16+ runners	60.5	50.5	102.8	83.9	47.4	42.1	64.7	66.5	50.8	88.6	85.1	115.1
Doncaster - all races	76.8	73.5	112.2	108.3	81.3	89.0	96.2	103.4	67.6	82.2	40.9	58.5
Up to 5 runners	107.8	103.5	57.0	57.0	53.8	43.1	0.0	0.0	825.0	645.0	0.0	0.0
6-10 runners	74.7	69.1	110.7	102.7	66.4	65.6	88.6	92.8	79.5	87.0	61.8	70.0
11-15 runners	46.5	46.1	88.4	92.1	92.6	103.7	143.5	151.9	80.0	89.9	39.8	89.1
16+ runners	88.1	85.7	138.8	134.5	102.4	125.4	93.3	104.7	46.4	69.5	38.2	49.3
Epsom - all races	104.2	96.3	96.1	97.1	124.4	130.8	33.3	30.7	63.7	80.5	35.5	61.2
Up to 5 runners	149.6	147.5	36.1	35.6	46.6	35.7	0.0	0.0	0.0	0.0	0.0	0.0
6-10 runners	89.3	82.1	114.3	126.1	84.8	93.9	53.7	51.1	91.9	107.8	0.0	0.0
11-15 runners	109.3	98.9	73.5	57.6	235.8	244.5	26.4	22.3	52.2	74.5	0.0	0.0
16+ runners	130.0	116.0	200.0	200.0	0.0	0.0	0.0	0.0	0.0	0.0	166.7	287.3
Goodwood - all races	101.5	101.3	67.8	64.0	81.8	77.8	82.8	95.3	71.9	79.6	64.6	82.0
Up to 5 runners	69.5	66.4	108.5	89.6	165.0	142.5	57.9	56.3	216.7	193.3	0.0	0.0
6-10 runners	99.5	101.9	67.3	62.8	54.2	54.4	58.1	75.8	80.0	96.7	110.3	109.4
11-15 runners	134.3	128.2	62.1	67.2	69.1	76.8	62.0	68.4	60.8	64.9	63.6	93.9
16+ runners	89.5	92.6	35.4	37.9	106.3	85.0	215.8	233.2	60.7	60.3	40.7	60.3
Newbury - all races	67.9	63.5	62.1	53.7	119.3	117.0	89.2	90.9	93.7	102.6	57.0	100.2
Up to 5 runners	96.6	91.9	39.3	30.0	96.4	90.0	63.6	70.0	460.0	492.0	0.0	0.0
6-10 runners	70.5	65.9	104.7	96.5	110.5	96.8	0.0	0.0	129.6	132.4	51.4	58.4
11-15 runners	67.9	66.3	38.3	31.7	129.2	124.4	113.6	117.6	66.6	77.9	58.6	95.9
16+ runners	49.4	41.7	45.5	35.8	129.0	145.2	193.8	192.5	84.0	92.8	58.4	113.7
Newmarket - all races	107.0	106.4	97.7	97.3	73.3	72.1	70.9	71.0	58.2	69.5	46.9	82.3
Up to 5 runners	76.0	72.8	98.6	91.1	75.0	60.6	125.0	113.3	0.0	0.0	0.0	0.0
6-10 runners	106.0	102.1	76.0	73.6	47.9	41.5	80.1	80.9	87.7	99.0	80.0	81.1
11-15 runners	120.1	123.2	111.2	110.0	107.5	107.8	40.4	33.7	54.3	69.2	17.7	24.8
16+ runners	100.6	103.6	125.7	133.2	76.9	92.6	81.6	92.4	31.2	37.2	50.7	120.2
York - all races	103.2	95.8	84.1	85.0	104.2	105.1	82.6	88.8	50.3	58.8	61.1	100.2
Up to 5 runners	116.4	110.0	70.8	61.7	73.1	77.7	0.0	0.0	0.0	0.0	0.0	0.0
6-10 runners	69.9	65.8	95.0	83.9	129.1	132.1	73.2	77.9	54.0	63.7	151.8	207.5
11-15 runners	110.3	104.3	96.1	114.4	70.5	58.2	136.9	158.8	43.0	47.6	32.4	73.0
16+ runners	134.5	120.0	50.0	48.0	127.8	138.9	58.8	46.5	59.9	73.0	49.7	83.0

Figures are based on an equal stake on every horse in each category.   Bold figures indicate the higher return

59

"Talking two-year-olds"

Legend

blank = no decision
(* =) = within 3lb.

Racehorse	Class (Down - Up + Same =)	Weight (Down - Up + Same =)	Form (Better - Worse + Same =*)	Decision (Down - Up + ##)

CLUNIE

Class	Weight	Form	Decision	Race number	Date	Racecourse	Race grade	Race type	Weight	Finishing position	Number of runners	Starting price	SP position	Notes
				1	19/8/98	Kempton	E	2yo Auction Maiden Stakes	8-4	15	18	20/1	6	
-	=	+		2	29/8/98	Windsor	F	2yo Selling Stakes	8-1	1	12	6/1	3	Tote paid £11.50
+	+	-	=	3	14/9/98	Nottingham	E	2yo Nursery (0-75)	8-6	1	19	5/1	1	
=	+	=		4	21/9/98	Leicester	E	2yo Nursery (0-75)	8-10	10	21	11/2	1	Formbook: 'half-hearted effort'
+	-	+		5	25/9/98	Haydock	D	2yo Nursery (0-85)	8-6	1	13	6/1	2	Formbook: explanation required
+	=	-		6	15/10/98	Newmarket	C	2yo Nursery	8-6	8	15	8/1	5	

Comment: this 2yo was found to be capable of winning a class D handicap and must have been a good bet in a seller, if true ability was known

DEHOUSH

Class	Weight	Form	Decision	Race number	Date	Racecourse	Race grade	Race type	Weight	Finishing position	Number of runners	Starting price	SP position	Notes
				1	26/6/98	Newmarket	D	2yo Maiden Stakes	9-0	1	13	10/1	5	Tote paid £17.20
++	=	-		2	9/7/98	Newmarket	A	2yo Stakes (Listed)	9-0	3	6	5/1	2	
-	=	=		3	29/9/98	Newmarket	B	2yo Conditions Stakes	9-0	9	26	8/1	4	

Comment: Insiders may have been confident of winning a class D maiden, when they had a horse capable of winning a class A race

HIT THE BEACH

Class	Weight	Form	Decision	Race number	Date	Racecourse	Race grade	Race type	Weight	Finishing position	Number of runners	Starting price	SP position	Notes
				1	8/5/98	Carlisle	D	2yo Maiden Stakes	9-0	9	9	16/1	6	Formbook: 'always well behind'
=	=	+		2	18/7/98	Ripon	D	2yo Maiden Stakes	9-0	1	14	7/2	3	Backed from 10/1, Tote paid £6.90
=	+	-		3	3/8/98	Ripon	D	2yo Novice Stakes	9-4	3	6	2/1	2	

Comment: Tote followers watching the odds would have known that this horse was being backed first time out at Ripon, but even so, the Tote dividend was outside the expected range.

HOUSTON TIME

Class	Weight	Form	Decision	Race number	Date	Racecourse	Race grade	Race type	Weight	Finishing position	Number of runners	Starting price	SP position	Notes
				1	16/9/98	Yarmouth	D	2yo Maiden Stakes	8-11	1	17	12/1	5	Horse opened 6/1, Tote paid £23.10
++	=	-		2	29/9/98	Newmarket	B	2yo Conditions Stakes	9-0	2	26	3/1	1	

Comment: This horse was only just caught in a good class B race at Newmarket, and the question is, what caused the low opening price at Yarmouth?

LADY ANGHARAD

Class	Weight	Form	Decision	Race number	Date	Racecourse	Race grade	Race type	Weight	Finishing position	Number of runners	Starting price	SP position	Notes
				1	25/5/98	Sandown	D	2yo fillies Maiden Stakes	8-11	4	10	8/1	5	
++	-	=		2	5/6/98	Epsom	A	2yo Stakes (Listed)	8-6	1	7	11/1	5	Tote paid £17.20
-	=	+	-	3	25/6/98	Salisbury	B	2yo Auction Stakes	8-6	1	11	11/10	1	
+	+	+	+	4	20/8/98	York	A	2yo fillies (Group 2)	8-11	8	10	20/1	6	
-	=	=		5	28/8/98	Goodwood	A	2yo fillies (Group 3)	8-12	5	9	11/1	3	
=	=	=		6	10/9/98	Doncaster	A	2yo fillies (Group 3)	8-12	7	10	16/1	6	
-	=	+		7	10/10/98	Ascot	A	2yo Stakes (Listed)	8-10	7	7	13/2	3	Price too low

Comment: In the Epsom race, bookmakers were operating to very small margins (105.3 in a 7 runner race=0.76 per runner), so the Tote dividend should have been well below starting price return.

"Talking two-year-olds" (continued)

```
## blank = no decision
(*~) = within 3lb.
```

Legend for Class / Weight / Form / Decision columns:
- Class: Down - / Up + / Same ~
- Weight: Down - / Up + / Same ~
- Form: Better - / Worse + / Same ~
- Decision: Down - / Up + / ##

PARISIEN STAR

Class	Weight	Form	Decision	Race number	Date	Racecourse	Race grade	Race type	Weight	Finishing position	Number of runners	Starting price	SP position	Notes
=	+	=		1	8/6/98	Windsor	E	2yo Maiden Auction Stakes	8-9	9	22	16/1	6	
=	+	-	=	2	22/6/98	Windsor	E	2yo Maiden Auction Stakes	9-0	15	24	16/1	6	
=	-	+	+	3	23/7/98	Sandown	E	2yo Maiden Auction Stakes	8-7	9	10	20/1	6	
+	+	+		4	18/8/98	Brighton	D	2yo Novice Stakes	8-12	3	7	33/1	6	
=	=	-		5	4/9/98	Epsom	D	2yo Nursery Handicap	8-13	1	9	11/2	2	Tote paid £9.10
+	=	=	+	6	18/9/98	Newbury	C	2yo Nursery Handicap	9-0	1	12	8/1	4	Tote paid £15.00
=	=	=		7	9/10/98	Ascot	C	2yo Nursery Handicap	9-2	2	15	9/1	5	Caught on the line, beaten a head.
=	-	=		8	30/10/98	Newmarket	C	2yo Conditions Stakes	8-11	4	13	8/1	5	

Comment: This horse was rated a 33/1 chance first time in a class D race and had previously never been in the betting in lower grade races. Suddenly, at Epsom, he is second favourite, and it is not surprising that Tote backers fail to catch up.

PETROVNA

Class	Weight	Form	Decision	Race number	Date	Racecourse	Race grade	Race type	Weight	Finishing position	Number of runners	Starting price	SP position	Notes
-	-	=		1	3/8/98	Windsor	D	2yo Maiden Stakes	8-11	5	18	50/1	6	
=	+	-	-	2	17/8/98	Windsor	E	2yo Maiden Auction Stakes	8-4	1	13	10/1	3	Tote paid £17.30
=	-	-	+	3	29/8/98	Windsor	E	2yo Novice Auction Stakes	8-13	5	11	5/1	3	Price down because of win
=	=	=	+	4	15/9/98	Sandown	D	2yo Nursery Handicap	8-10	2	12	6/1	3	
++	=	-	+	5	29/9/98	Newmarket	B	2yo Nursery Handicap	8-10	13	13	16/1	6	

Comment: A student of form could have selected this horse when she won. On her debut she had finished a creditable fifth, and now she was back on the same course, down in class and down in weight. The SP-Tote gap suggested the latter offered value.

RED PRAIRIE

Class	Weight	Form	Decision	Race number	Date	Racecourse	Race grade	Race type	Weight	Finishing position	Number of runners	Starting price	SP position	Notes
=	=	=		1	24/4/98	Carlisle	D	2yo Maiden Stakes	9-0	9	18	10/1	5	
=	=	-	=	2	3/5/98	Hamilton	D	2yo Maiden Stakes	9-0	1	7	5/2	2	Jockey suspended for excessive whip use
+	=	=		3	22/5/98	Pontefract	C	2yo Conditions Stakes	9-1	1	5	2/1	2	
++	=	=	+	4	16/6/98	Ascot (Royal)	A	2yo Stakes (Group 3)	8-12	8	17	20/1	6	
=	=	=		5	17/7/98	San Siro (Italy)	A	2yo Stakes (Group 3)	8-11	3	9	not known	nk	
-	=	=		6	19/8/98	York	A	2yo cdlg (Listed)	8-11	1	7	11/2	4	Tote paid £10.70
++	=	-		7	12/9/98	Doncaster	A	2yo Stakes (Group 2)	8-11	3	13	11/2	2	
-	=	=	-	8	10/9/98	Ascot	A	2yo Stakes (Group 3)	8-12	6	12	7/1	4	Price a little high

Comment: The low price of 11/2 at York seemed difficult to justify, given his previous price of 20/1 in a UK grade A race.

ROSE OF MOONCOIN

Class	Weight	Form	Decision	Race number	Date	Racecourse	Race grade	Race type	Weight	Finishing position	Number of runners	Starting price	SP position	Notes
+++	-	-		1	6/6/98	Newmarket	D	2yo Maiden (f) Stakes	8-11	1	9	10/1	4	Tote paid £21.70
=	=	=	-	2	7/7/98	Newmarket	A	2yo fillies Stakes (Group 2)	8-9	4	10	10/1	5	
-		=		3	25/7/98	Ascot	A	2yo fillies Stakes (Group 3)	8-9	5	6	7/1	3	

Comment: It is not difficult to understand why this horse was backed to win her class D maiden, as connections would have known that she was destined to run in the highest grade races.

UNDETERRED

Class	Weight	Form	Decision	Race number	Date	Racecourse	Race grade	Race type	Weight	Finishing position	Number of runners	Starting price	SP position	Notes
=	=	=		1	15/7/98	Folkestone	D	2yo Maiden Stakes	9-0	4	13	14/1	5	
=	=	=		2	20/8/98	Yarmouth	D	2yo Maiden Stakes	9-0	1	7	6/1	2	Dead-heat
+	=	+		3	17/9/98	Yarmouth	C	2yo Conditions Stakes	9-1	4	8	25/1	6	Price too high (market warning)
++	-	+	+	4	10/10/98	York	A	2yo Stakes (Listed)	8-11	1	11	14/1	5	Tote paid £48.90

Comment: When this horse moved up one notch to a class C race, his odds went up to 25/1, and although these odds seemed low, 33/1 would have seemed appropriate for a class A race. Accordingly 14/1 at York must raise eyebrows.

Seasoned racers

## blank = no decision (* =) = within 3lb.	Down - Up + Same =	Down - Up + Same =*	Better - Worse + Same =	Down - Up + ##

Racehorse	Class	Weight	Form	Decision	Race number	Date	Racecourse

RAIVE

Class	Weight	Form	Decision	Race number	Date	Racecourse
				1	16/10/96	Haydock
=	=	+		2	29/5/97	Carlisle
-	=	-	-	3	19/6/97	Ripon
+	=	-		4	19/7/97	Ayr
=/+	=	=		5	10/9/97	Doncaster
=/-	+	+		6	6/10/97	Pontefract
=/+	=	+	+	7	18/10/97	Redcar
+	=	=		8	16/8/98	Ripon
-	+	=		9	22/8/98	Ripon
+	-	-		10	11/9/98	Doncaster
-	+	+		11	21/9/98	Kempton

Comment: Raive showed good early form in 1997, but deteriation was accompanied by the odds in his races going steadfily outwards. By the first race in 1998, the bookmakers appeared to be confident of failure by offering long odds and his finishing position, seventh out of ten, gradually weakening two furlongs out, confirmed their view.

SILKEN DALLIANCE

Class	Weight	Form	Decision	Race number	Date	Racecourse
				1	23/9/97	Nottingham
-	=	+		2	4/10/97	Wolverhampton (AW)
=	=	-		3	28/10/97	Leicester
+	=	=		4	21/2/98	Wolverhampton (AW)
-	=	-	-	5	20/3.98	Southwell (AW)
++	-	=		6	27/6/98	Bath
-	=	=		7	18/7/98	Nottingham
+	-	=		8	9/8/98	Epsom
-	+	+		9	9/9/98	Kempton
++	-	-		10	19/9/98	Newbury
+	-	+		11	27/9/98	Ascot
-	++	-		12	17/10/98	Newmarket

Comment: Silken Dalliance failed to win a class F race in 1997, yet started odds on to win a class D race at Wolverhampton, and might have won had she not met interference. However, by mid-1998 the form was suggesting that she may be a good class D handicapper, and this view appeared to hold good when she failed in a class C handicap at Epsom off bottom weight of 7st7lb and then won a class D handicap at Kempton with plenty in hand. It did not come as a surpridse, therefore, when she fin-

Race grade	Race type	Weight	Finishing position	Number of runners	Starting price	SP position	Notes
D	2yo Maiden	9-0	7	10	16/1	6	
D	3yo Maiden Stakes	8-12	2	10	50/1	3	Joint third favourite at 50/1!
E	3yo Auction Maiden Stakes	9-0	1	12	6/1	3	
D	3yo Limited Stakes (0-80)	9-1	3	7	8/1	4	Beaten only a head and short head
D	3yo Limited Stakes (0-85)	8-13	6	12	10/1	5	
D	3yo Handicap (0-80)	9-7	13	14	10/1	5	
D	3yo+ Handicap (0-85)	9-6	10	16	20/1	6	
C	3yo+ Handicap (0-90)	9-5	7	10	40/1	6	
D	3yo+ Handicap (0-85)	9-9	1	8	8/1	5	Tote paid £16.80
C	3yo+ Handicap (0-100)	9-0	6	17	14/1	5	
D	3yo+ Class'd Stakes (0-85)	9-7	6	6	8/1	5	Highest price in race

However, the Raceform race reader noted, 'a useful sort who looks made for jumping, ran a fair first race of the season and should improve for it'. Just six days later on the same racecourse the prediction came true and Raive won easing up. However, as the odds had tumbled from 40/1 in his previous race to 8/1, the market did not appear to be surprised.

Race grade	Race type	Weight	Finishing position	Number of runners	Starting price	SP position	Notes
D	2yo fillies Maiden Stakes	8-11	10	18	20/1	6	
F	2yo Auction Maiden Stakes	8-9	2	13	10/1	5	
F	2yo Auction Maiden Stakes	8-9	4	21	9/1	5	
D	3yo Maiden Stakes	8-9	2	9	4/6	1	Odds on not justified. Met interference.
F	3yo Auction Maiden Stakes	8-9	1	11	4/5	1	
C	3yo Handicap (0-90)	8-1	5	9	6/1	3	
D	3yo Handicap (0-85)	8-3	2	6	15/2	5	
C	3yo+ Handicap (0-95)	7-7	7	12	14/1	5	
D	3yo Handicap (0-75)	9-0	1	18	7/1	4	Formbook: 'won with plenty in hand'
C	3yo+ Handicap (0-100)	8-10	17	19	9/1	3	Price too short (due to previous win)
B	3yo+ Handicap	7-7	1	24	10/1	3	Tote paid £16.40
B	3yo+ Handicap	9-1	1	30	8/1	3	

ished 17th of 19 in a class C handicap, rated 0-100 carrying 8st10lb. The Ascot Stewards apparently did not hold this view for, while they accepted that she was entitled to win a class B handicap carrying 7st 7lb, they did not accept that this correlated with the Newbury run. Clearly the Ascot Stewards were correct because Silken Dalliance followed up her Ascot win in a class B handicap (£37,000 added) at Newmarket, despite being up 22lb in the weights. The transition from winning a class F auction maiden stakes to carrying more than 9st to victory in a top class B handicap was

blank = no decision
(* =) = within 3lb.

	Down - Up + Same =	Down - Up + Same =*	Better - Worse + Same =	Down - Up + ##
Class	Weight	Form	Decision	

ROYAL RESULT

Class	Weight	Form	Decision	Race number	Date	Racecourse	Race grade
=	+	=		1	8/4/96	Kempton	D
=	=	-		2	18/4/96	Ripon	D
=	=	-		3	25/7/96	Sandown	D
+	-	-		4	2/8/96	Thirsk	D
=/-	+	+		5	13/9/96	Goodwood	C
-	=	=		6	29/9/96	Hamilton	C
-	=	=		7	17/10/96	Redcar	D
++	=	=	+	8	21/3/97	Doncaster	B
-	-	+		9	31/3/97	Kempton	C
-	+	=		10	25/4/97	Carlisle	D
+	-	=		11	3/5/97	Thirsk	C
-	=	=		12	10/5/97	Beverley	D
=/-	+	=		13	23/8/97	Redcar	D
=/-	=	=/-	-	14	4/9/97	York	D
+	-	+		15	19/9/97	Ayr	C
=	=	-	=/-	16	4/10/97	Newmarket	C
-	+	-		17	28/10/97	Redcar	D
++	=	+	+	18	27/3/98	Doncaster	B
-	-	+		19	2/5/98	Thirsk	C
-	=	=		20	9/5/98	Beverley	D
-	+	+		21	2/6/98	Beverley	E
++	-	=		22	10/7/98	York	C
-	+	=		23	16/7/98	Doncaster	D
-	=	-	-	24	24/7/98	Thirsk	E
+	=	=		25	9/8/98	Redcar	D
-	+	=		26	14/8/98	Catterick	E
++	-	-		27	25/8/98	Pontefract	C
-	+	+		28	3/9/98	York	D
+	-	-		29	10/9/98	Doncaster	C
+	-	+		30	19/9/98	Ayr	B
--	+	-		31	27/9/98	Musselburgh	D

Comment: *Royal Result was trained by M. R. Stoute in 1996 and in that year made steady progress, which was noted in the Form Book. His one win that year hardly came as a surprise, given his odds were 1/5. By the beginning of 1997 he had moved to T. D. Barron but, after seven races without success, he moved to M. W. Easterby in September. In his second race for his new trainer, at Newmarket, he was clear third favourite in the betting for a class C race, but had never before been in the betting in that class of race, when running in big fields. However, the market got it right for, despite being unruly in the stalls, he won very easily. Royal Result's third trainer could not conjure up any more*

Race type	Weight	Finishing position	Number of runners	Starting price	SP position	Notes
3yo+ Maiden Stakes	8-12	8	16	20/1	6	
3yo Maiden Stakes	9-0	5	14	10/1	5	Formbook: open to further improvement
3yo+ Maiden Stakes	8-13	2	12	14/1	4	Formbook: race waiting for him
3yo+ Maiden Stakes	8-12	1	7	1/5	1	
3yo+ H'cap 0-100	8-8	12	17	12/1	5	
3yo+ H'cap 0-90	9-10	4	8	4/1	1	
3yo+ H'cap 0-85	9-10	3	13	8/1	5	
4yo+ Handicap	9-9	16	23	14/1	5	
4yo+ H'cap 0-95	9-1	11	20	12/1	5	
3yo+ H'cap 0-85	9-8	6	12	11/2	3	FB: gelded, after being sold for 33,000 guineas
3yo+ H'cap 0-90	9-0	8	17	9/1	5	
3yo+ H'cap 0-85	9-1	6	19	16/1	6	
3yo+ H'cap 0-80	9-8	5	13	10/1	5	
3yo + H'cap 0-75	9-8	16	22	10/1	5	
3yo+ H'cap 0-90	8-6	4	18	16/1	6	
3yo+ H'cap 0-90	8-5	1	24	7/1	3	Tote paid £15.20
3yo+ H'cap 0-85	9-3	5	15	9/4	1	
4yo+ Handicap	9-3	13	24	16/1	6	
3yo+ H'cap 0-90	8-12	7	18	33/1	6	12/1 for this race previous year
3yo+ H'cap 0-85	9-0	12	18	12/1	5	
3yo+ H'cap 0-70	9-7	3	12	10/1	5	
3yo+ H'cap 0-90	8-7	7	12	7/1	4	Price too low (see race 19)
3yo+ H'cap 0-75	9-9	4	17	7/1	2	
3yo+ H'cap 0-70	9-9	3	10	7/4	1	
3yo+ H'cap 0-75	9-7	6	14	11/2	4	
3yo+ H'cap 0-70	9-11	2	20	7/1	3	
3yo+ H'cap 0-90	8-13	8	12	11/1	5	
3yo+ H'cap 0-75	9-11	1	24	12/1	5	Tote paid £27.70
3yo+ H'cap 0-90	9-2	4	20	6/1	1	
3yo+ Handicap	8-12	1	29	12/1	4	(Tote paid £14.70 - in line)
3yo+ H'cap 0-85	9-11	9	13	7/2	1	

wins so, in the summer of 1998 he was off again, this time to D. Nicholls. A fresh environment seems to encourage the horse and he was soon winning, but again victory was anticipated in the market, although, set against this, there was evidence of market moves on other occasions when the horse did not win. Royal Result is a clear example, therefore, that 'insider trading' is not risk free, and merely reflects superior knowledge, rather than any form of skulduggery. Note that after most of his wins he was made clear favourite next time out, but he never managed two consecutive wins.

Table 3-8   Analysis of betting returns   1998

	Percentage of stake returned										
	Favourite		Second favourite		Third favourite		Fourth favourite		Odds to 14/1 (SP)		Odds 16/1+ (SP)	
	SP	Tote	SP	Tote	SP	Tote	SP	Tote	SP	Tote	SP	Tote
Ascot - all races	93.4	81.6	113.1	114.0	92.4	94.1	113.9	111.0	62.5	74.1	51.3	52.5
Up to 5 runners	0.0	0.0	196.4	198.6	178.6	147.1	130.0	98.0	0.0	0.0	0.0	0.0
6-10 runners	110.6	98.7	82.6	71.3	110.8	105.7	125.0	123.8	20.9	25.7	114.1	104.5
11-15 runners	142.0	114.3	75.0	79.2	56.7	56.7	0.0	0.0	128.6	151.8	30.4	53.0
16+ runners	67.7	60.6	159.3	178.5	55.0	82.0	157.7	156.5	63.6	75.1	40.1	39.2
Doncaster - all races	101.9	98.2	73.6	69.1	57.7	62.2	63.6	61.4	54.3	77.3	67.2	104.2
Up to 5 runners	108.6	100.6	85.2	86.9	0.0	0.0	187.5	161.3	0.0	0.0	0.0	0.0
6-10 runners	103.4	98.8	53.4	46.9	67.9	68.5	88.9	94.3	71.3	88.8	60.0	56.4
11-15 runners	107.9	104.8	163.0	144.3	131.0	141.0	0.0	0.0	40.8	65.8	30.4	62.6
16+ runners	93.5	92.4	51.8	54.3	17.8	24.7	46.4	39.5	51.3	77.6	80.0	126.8
Epsom - all races	67.2	58.1	126.9	122.4	56.7	53.3	100.0	85.3	93.5	107.3	65.0	77.0
Up to 5 runners	100.1	100.0	145.8	135.0	0.0	0.0	180.0	120.0	0.0	0.0	0.0	0.0
6-10 runners	80.2	67.9	143.8	140.4	23.2	28.2	92.9	85.4	106.9	116.0	60.5	67.0
11-15 runners	37.0	30.8	73.7	65.8	108.6	95.9	112.5	95.6	94.5	116.2	91.6	111.0
16+ runners	112.5	95.0	200.0	208.3	0.0	0.0	0.0	0.0	52.6	44.2	0.0	0.0
Goodwood - all races	107.1	105.4	108.3	96.8	40.6	38.6	79.0	83.6	67.5	75.8	50.3	87.8
Up to 5 runners	142.1	136.8	102.6	67.9	20.6	21.0	78.6	85.7	0.0	0.0	0.0	0.0
6-10 runners	109.8	106.7	112.6	105.0	73.3	67.9	32.4	32.2	58.3	62.1	58.1	53.1
11-15 runners	46.4	41.3	138.3	124.7	22.2	23.7	117.6	128.9	69.5	84.1	75.2	105.8
16+ runners	143.5	151.1	56.8	57.3	0.0	0.0	121.2	125.4	75.7	82.9	36.0	99.3
Newbury - all races	79.8	72.1	95.3	90.5	101.7	98.2	100.0	111.9	52.9	59.1	76.5	129.4
Up to 5 runners	94.3	97.7	155.2	130.9	87.5	67.5	70.0	79.0	0.0	0.0	0.0	0.0
6-10 runners	83.7	75.3	80.3	72.1	106.0	102.8	53.3	61.7	80.2	90.6	79.2	130.2
11-15 runners	61.5	54.7	89.2	84.1	91.4	97.4	207.7	235.0	39.8	43.0	116.4	197.1
16+ runners	87.6	74.6	97.9	107.1	126.5	114.7	50.0	50.0	55.2	63.3	56.0	95.2
Newmarket - all races	89.5	89.6	95.1	92.3	53.5	53.5	67.8	74.4	86.2	100.8	58.7	73.8
Up to 5 runners	108.2	107.1	44.3	39.5	62.5	66.0	211.1	200.0	0.0	0.0	94.4	78.3
6-10 runners	77.9	73.2	83.8	76.4	68.1	64.6	47.1	57.3	103.6	107.7	145.8	137.3
11-15 runners	94.4	94.2	90.2	91.5	60.2	64.2	103.0	105.8	70.0	82.8	64.2	90.9
16+ runners	96.1	104.4	141.2	142.5	17.3	17.3	34.5	42.7	88.7	114.5	36.2	52.4
York - all races	99.0	92.8	68.6	63.4	103.3	97.1	130.4	151.4	56.4	85.8	45.9	68.5
Up to 5 runners	85.8	75.3	135.0	120.7	150.0	153.3	0.0	0.0	0.0	0.0	0.0	0.0
6-10 runners	119.5	111.4	57.4	57.0	73.0	60.8	154.1	182.2	27.9	28.4	110.0	137.6
11-15 runners	102.3	102.3	45.8	37.9	143.8	121.3	42.1	48.4	91.1	139.5	23.3	37.0
16+ runners	82.0	75.7	67.9	63.1	101.3	104.3	211.5	241.2	49.7	80.0	41.4	65.8

Figures are based on an equal stake on every horse in each category.   Bold figures indicate the higher return

66

Table 3-9 Table recommending betting medium to maximise potential returns

Each betting-medium column below is divided into four runner-size boxes arranged:
`2-5 runners | 6-10 runners` (top) and `11-15 runners | 16+ runners` (bottom). Shading is indicated as (plain), (light) or (dark) per the Key.

Grade of race	Favourite	Second favourite	Third favourite	Fourth favourite	Odds to 14/1 (SP)	Odds 16/1+ (SP)
A	2-5 runners (plain), 6-10 runners (plain), 11-15 runners (plain), 16+ runners (dark)	2-5 runners (plain), 6-10 runners (plain), 11-15 runners (plain), 16+ runners (plain)	2-5 runners (plain), 6-10 runners (plain), 11-15 runners (plain), 16+ runners (light)	2-5 runners (plain), 6-10 runners (plain), 11-15 runners (plain), 16+ runners (plain)	2-5 runners (light), 6-10 runners (plain), 11-15 runners (light), 16+ runners (light)	2-5 runners (light), 6-10 runners (light), 11-15 runners (light), 16+ runners (dark)
B	2-5 runners (plain), 6-10 runners (plain), 11-15 runners (light), 16+ runners (dark)	2-5 runners (plain), 6-10 runners (light), 11-15 runners (light), 16+ runners (light)	2-5 runners (plain), 6-10 runners (plain), 11-15 runners (light), 16+ runners (dark)	2-5 runners (plain), 6-10 runners (plain), 11-15 runners (light), 16+ runners (light)	2-5 runners (light), 6-10 runners (light), 11-15 runners (light), 16+ runners (light)	2-5 runners (light), 6-10 runners (light), 11-15 runners (light), 16+ runners (dark)
C	2-5 runners (plain), 6-10 runners (plain), 11-15 runners (plain), 16+ runners (plain)	2-5 runners (plain), 6-10 runners (plain), 11-15 runners (plain), 16+ runners (plain)	2-5 runners (plain), 6-10 runners (plain), 11-15 runners (light), 16+ runners (light)	2-5 runners (plain), 6-10 runners (light), 11-15 runners (light), 16+ runners (light)	2-5 runners (light), 6-10 runners (light), 11-15 runners (light), 16+ runners (light)	2-5 runners (light), 6-10 runners (light), 11-15 runners (light), 16+ runners (dark)
D	2-5 runners (plain), 6-10 runners (plain), 11-15 runners (light), 16+ runners (dark)	2-5 runners (plain), 6-10 runners (light), 11-15 runners (light), 16+ runners (light)	2-5 runners (plain), 6-10 runners (plain), 11-15 runners (light), 16+ runners (dark)	2-5 runners (plain), 6-10 runners (light), 11-15 runners (light), 16+ runners (light)	2-5 runners (light), 6-10 runners (light), 11-15 runners (light), 16+ runners (light)	2-5 runners (light), 6-10 runners (light), 11-15 runners (light), 16+ runners (dark)
E to G	2-5 runners (dark), 6-10 runners (light), 11-15 runners (dark), 16+ runners (dark)	2-5 runners (light), 6-10 runners (light), 11-15 runners (light), 16+ runners (light)	2-5 runners (light), 6-10 runners (light), 11-15 runners (light), 16+ runners (dark)	2-5 runners (light), 6-10 runners (light), 11-15 runners (light), 16+ runners (light)	2-5 runners (light), 6-10 runners (light), 11-15 runners (light), 16+ runners (light)	2-5 runners (light), 6-10 runners (light), 11-15 runners (light), 16+ runners (dark)

Key:

Unshaded box recommends backing with bookmakers, as starting price returns should exceed Tote dividends.

Lightly shaded box suggests that starting price returns and Tote dividends should be very close and it will be difficult to predict which comes out the better.

Dark shaded box recommends backing with the Tote, as Tote dividends should exceed starting price returns. Very dark boxes may return vastly superior Tote dividends.

Raceform rating	Average winning rating	Racehorse	Trainer	Number of runs	Number of wins	Winning %	Position in the betting, when winning			
106	1.0	ABREEZE (USA)	Suroor, S bin	3	1	33.3	1			
98	2.3	ACE OF PARKES	Berry, J	7	3	42.9	2	3	2	
90	1.5	ACICULA	Johnstone, M	7	2	28.6	0	3		
94	2.0	AGINOR	Cecil, H R A	5	2	40.0	1	3		
93	0.0	AGREEABLE	Loder, D R	1	1	100.0	0			
93	0.0	AKARITA	McMahon, B A	8	1	12.5	0			
122	2.0	ALBORADA	Prescott, Sir Mark	4	3	75.0	1	2	3	
105	1.8	ALCAZAR	Dunlop, J L	8	4	50.0	2	3	1	1
112	0.7	ALJABR (USA)	Suroor, S bin	3	3	100.0	1	0	1	
110	3.0	ALMATY (IRE)	Muir, W R	9	2	22.2	1	5		
99	1.5	ALMOND ROCK	Fanshawe, J R	12	2	16.7	1	2		
121	2.0	ALMUSHTARAK (IRE)	Kelleway, Miss Gay	11	1	9.1	2			
105	0.5	ALTAWEELAH (IRE)	Cumani, L M	7	2	28.6	1	0		
96	0.5	AL WAFFI	Loder, D R	3	2	66.7	1	0		
102	4.3	ALWAYS ALIGHT	Burke, K R	12	3	25.0	5	2	6	
92	0.0	ALYRIVA (USA)	Loder, D R	2	1	50.0	0			
95	2.3	AMAZING DREAM (IRE)	Hannon, R	7	3	42.9	3	2	2	
93	3.5	AMERICAN WHISPER	Harris, P W	3	2	66.7	5	2		
123	1.0	AMONG MEN	Stoute, Sir Michael	7	2	28.6	0	2		
119	2.5	ANDREYEV (IRE)	Hannon, R	8	2	25.0	3	2		
92	0.0	ANNO DOMINI	Cole, P F I	4	1	25.0	0			
122	1.0	ANNUS MIRABILIS (FR)	Suroor, S bin	1	1	100.0	1			
93	3.0	ANOTHER TIME	Woods, S P C	14	2	14.3	5	1		
97	1.0	APACHE RED (IRE)	Elsworth, D R C	6	1	16.7	1			
112	6.0	APPREHENSION	Loder, D R	4	1	25.0	6			
120	2.3	ARCTIC OWL	Fanshawe, J R	4	3	75.0	4	1	2	
106	6.0	ARRIVING	Hills, J W	5	1	20.0	6			
102	0.0	ASAD	Suroor, S bin	2	1	50.0	0			
92	6.0	ASCOT CYCLONE (USA)	Hills, B W	6	1	16.7	6			
106	2.5	ASHRAAKAT (USA)	Dunlop, J L	8	2	25.0	2	3		
95	3.0	ASTRAC	Nicholls, D	9	2	22.2	2	4		
99	3.0	ATLANTIC DESTINY	Johnstone, M	7	2	28.6	3	3		
111	1.3	AUCTION HOUSE	Hills, B W	5	3	60.0	0	2	2	
116	1.5	BAHR	Suroor, S bin	6	2	33.3	2	1		
104	0.0	BALLET MASTER	Cecil, H R A	1	1	100.0	0			
99	2.0	BALTIC STATE	Cecil, H R A	3	1	33.3	2			
92	0.0	BARAFAMY	Dunlop, J L	4	1	25.0	0			
96	1.0	BAWSAIN	Eyre, J L	10	2	20.0	1	1		
93	1.0	BEAT ALL	Stoute, Sir Michael	2	1	50.0	1			
108	6.0	BEAUCHAMP KING	Butler, G A	5	1	20.0	6			
96	1.0	BENIN	Cecil, H R A	5	1	20.0	1			
111	1.5	BERAYSIM	Jarvis, M A	7	2	28.6	2	1		
102	0.0	BERLIOZ	Loder, D R	2	1	50.0	0			
104	2.0	BERTOLINI	Gosden, J H M	6	1	16.7	2			
100	6.0	BE THE CHIEF	Mills, T G	2	1	50.0	6			
102	2.0	BIENAMADO (USA)	Chapple-Hyam, P W	2	1	50.0	2			
110	1.3	BINT ALLAYL	Channon, M R	4	3	75.0	2	1	1	
103	2.0	BIONIC	Cecil, H R A	1	1	100.0	2			
116	1.0	BISHOPS COURT	Ramsden, Mrs J R	12	2	16.7	1	1		

Raceform rating	Average winning rating	Racehorse	Trainer	Number of runs	Number of wins	Winning %	Position in the betting, when winning			
99	2.0	BLACK AMBER	Callaghan, N A	3	1	33.3	2			
100	2.5	BLESSINGINDISGUISE	Easterby, M W	7	2	28.6	4	1		
105	1.0	BLUE MELODY	Loder, D R	4	1	25.0	1			
110	3.0	BOLD EDGE	Hannon, R	8	3	37.5	2	5	2	
95	3.5	BOLD EFFORT	Cunningham-Brown, K O	7	2	28.6	3	4		
113	1.0	BOLD FACT	Cecil, H R A	5	2	40.0	1	1		
98	4.7	BOLDLY GOES	Fairhurst, C W	4	3	75.0	6	3	5	
106	3.0	BOLLIN JOANNE	Easterby, T D	6	1	16.7	3			
120	3.7	BOLSHOI	Berry, J	7	3	42.9	1	5	5	
100	2.0	BON AMI	Berry, J	12	3	25.0	2	2	2	
99	4.5	BOOMERANG BLADE	Smart, B	5	2	40.0	3	6		
119	2.0	BORDER ARROW	Balding I A	4	1	25.0	2			
104	0.5	BRANCASTER	Chapple-Hyam, P W	2	2	100.0	0	1		
100	4.0	BRAVE EDGE	Hannon, R	13	1	7.7	4			
98	1.0	BRAVE REWARD	Stoute, Sir Michael	6	1	16.7	1			
96	2.0	BRIEF ESCAPADE	Chapple-Hyam, P W	3	1	33.3	2			
95	5.0	BRILLIANT RED	Hedger, P R	6	1	16.7	5			
104	1.0	BRIMMING	Cecil, H R A	7	3	42.9	1	1	1	
107	1.5	BRISTOL CHANNEL	Hills, B W	4	2	50.0	1	2		
105	3.5	BRYONY BRIND	Fanshawe, J R	6	2	33.3	6	1		
119	1.0	BUSY FLIGHT	Hills, B W	4	1	25.0	1			
100	1.0	CABALLERO	Brittain, C E	6	1	16.7	1			
93	3.8	CADEAUX CHER	Hills, B W	16	4	25.0	5	0	4	6
98	2.5	CALANDO	Loder, D R	4	2	50.0	4	1		
121	6.0	CAPE CROSS	Gosden, J H M	5	1	20.0	6			
92	6.0	CAPE GRACE	Hannon, R	3	1	33.3	6			
124	1.0	CAPE VERDI	Suroor, S bin	2	1	50.0	1			
113	1.0	CAPRI	Cecil, H R A	6	3	50.0	1	0	2	
91	0.0	CAPTAIN LOGAN	Loder, D R	4	1	25.0	0			
100	3.5	CARIBBEAN MONARCH	Stoute, Sir Michael	3	2	66.7	5	2		
97	2.0	CARRANITA	Palling, B	14	1	7.1	2			
103	2.5	CASINO CAPTIVE	Chapple-Hyam, P W	5	2	40.0	5	0		
115	2.0	CATCHASCATCHCAN	Cecil, H R A	4	4	100.0	1	5	1	1
113	5.0	CATHEDRAL	Meehan, B J	6	1	16.7	5			
92	0.5	CHATTING	Stoute, Sir Michael	3	2	66.7	1	0		
121	0.5	CHESTER HOUSE	Cecil, H R A	7	2	28.6	1	0		
92	4.0	CHEWIT	Moore, G L	9	1	11.1	4			
93	2.7	CHEYENNE GOLD	Hannon, R	6	3	50.0	3	0	5	
94	3.0	CHIEF REBEL	Wragg, G	3	1	33.3	3			
104	2.0	CHIST	Tompkins, M H	3	1	33.3	2			
91	4.0	CHOMPER	Channon, M R	14	1	7.1	4			
104	2.3	CHURLISH CHARM	Hannon, R	5	3	60.0	3	1	3	
99	0.0	CIRCLE OF GOLD	Chapple-Hyam, P W	4	2	50.0	0	0		
105	3.0	CLAPHAM COMMON	Cumani, L M	3	1	33.3	3			
93	3.0	CLASSY CLEO	Evans, P D	17	3	17.6	4	2	6	
109	2.0	CLERKENWELL	Stoute, Sir Michael	5	1	20.0	2			
115	6.0	CLOUD CASTLE	Brittain, C E	8	1	12.5	6			
90	3.0	COLLEVILLE	Jarvis, M A	7	2	28.6	3	3		
110	1.5	COMMANDER COLLINS	Chapple-Hyam, P W	3	2	66.7	0	1		
96	2.0	COMPTON ADMIRAL	Butler, G A	4	1	25.0	2			
95	4.5	COMPTON ARROW (IRE)	Butler, G A	6	2	33.3	5	4		

69

Raceform rating	Average winning rating	Racehorse	Trainer	Number of runs	Number of wins	Winning %	Position in the betting. when winning			
91	1.5	CONFIDANTE	Stoute, Sir Michael	8	2	25.0	2	1		
101	0.0	CONNOISSEUR BAY	Chapple-Hyam, P W	3	1	33.3	0			
90	2.0	CORNICHE	Cole, P F I	5	1	20.0	2			
104	1.5	CORTACHY CASTLE (IRE)	Meehan, B J	7	2	28.6	0	3		
116	4.0	COURTEOUS	Cole, P F I	5	1	20.0	4			
115	3.5	CRAIGSTEEL	Cecil, H R A	3	2	66.7	5	2		
116	2.0	CRIMSON TIDE	Hills, J W	5	1	20.0	2			
94	2.0	CRUMPTON HILL	Graham, N A	9	1	11.1	2			
95	2.0	CUGINA	Balding, G B	7	1	14.3	2			
94	1.0	CYBINKA	Hannon, R	3	1	33.3	1			
92	5.0	CYRIAN	Cole, P F I	6	1	16.7	5			
98	2.0	DALIAPOUR (IRE)	Cumani, L M	4	2	50.0	2	2		
99	0.0	DANCING PHANTOM	Stoute, Sir Michael	3	1	33.3	0			
115	2.5	DANISH RHAPSODY (IRE)	Herries, Lady	10	2	20.0	3	2		
103	0.0	DARING DEREK (USA)	Loder, D R	3	1	33.3	0			
98	2.0	DARING DESTINY	Burke, K R	7	1	14.3	2			
111	2.5	DARK MOONDANCER	Chapple-Hyam, P W	4	2	50.0	2	3		
113	4.0	DARK SHELL (IRE)	Stoute, Sir Michael	5	1	20.0	4			
100	2.0	DARNAWAY	Cecil, H R A	3	1	33.3	2			
99	3.0	DATO STAR (IRE)	Jefferson, J M	5	1	20.0	3			
101	3.0	DAUNTING LADY (IRE)	Hannon, R	7	1	14.3	3			
123	1.0	DAYLAMI (IRE)	Suroor, S bin	5	2	40.0	1	1		
102	1.5	DEADLY NIGHTSHADE (IRE)	Elsworth, D R C	3	2	66.7	2	1		
121	1.7	DECORATED HERO	Gosden, J H M	5	3	60.0	2	1	2	
102	3.0	DEEP DIVE (USA)	Cole, P F I	4	1	25.0	3			
91	5.0	DEHOUSH (USA)	Stewart, A C	3	1	33.3	5			
111	5.0	DELILAH (IRE)	Stoute, Sir Michael	6	1	16.7	5			
99	2.0	DESARU (USA)	Noseda, J	3	1	33.3	2			
129	3.5	DESERT PRINCE (IRE)	Loder, D R	7	4	57.1	5	4	4	1
100	0.0	DESIGNER (USA)	Gosden, J H M	3	1	33.3	0			
95	4.0	DIAMOND WHITE	Wingrove, K G	17	2	11.8	3	5		
112	3.0	DIGITALIZE (USA)	Cecil, H R A	6	2	33.3	5	1		
118	1.0	DIKTAT	Loder, D R	4	3	75.0	1	1	1	
111	2.0	DOCKSIDER (USA)	Hills, J W	5	1	20.0	2			
93	1.5	DOCTOR SPIN (IRE)	Johnson-Houghton, R F	3	2	66.7	2	1		
90	2.0	DOLLAR LAW	Cole, P F I	3	1	33.3	2			
97	0.0	DOOMNA (IRE)	Suroor, S bin	3	1	33.3	0			
104	2.0	DOUBLE CLASSIC (USA)	Stoute, Sir Michael	4	3	75.0	3	2	1	
120	1.5	DOUBLE TRIGGER (IRE)	Johnston, M	5	2	40.0	2	1		
105	5.0	DOVEDON STAR	Kellaway, A	9	1	11.1	5			
101	5.0	DOWER HOUSE	Jarvis, W	5	1	20.0	5			
93	4.5	DRAMATIZE (IRE)	Meehan, B J	8	2	25.0	6	3		
90	3.7	EASTERN LYRIC	Berry, J	9	3	33.3	3	6	2	
106	5.0	EASTERN PURPLE (IRE)	Fahey, R A	10	1	10.0	5			
115	3.5	EASYCALL	Meehan, B J	10	2	20.0	2	5		
107	3.5	EATON SQUARE (USA)	Cecil, H R A	3	2	66.7	6	1		
95	3.0	ELHAYQ (IRE)	Dunlop, J L	7	1	14.3	3			
95	0.0	ELHIDA (IRE)	Tregoning, M P	3	1	33.3	0			

70

Raceform rating	Average winning rating	Racehorse	Trainer	Number of runs	Number of wins	Winning %	Position in the betting, when winning			
125	1.0	ELNADIM (USA)	Dunlop, J L	5	1	20.0	1			
95	2.0	EL TANGO	Meehan, B J	4	1	25.0	2			
96	0.5	ELTAWAASUL (USA)	Dunlop, J L	4	2	50.0	1	0		
99	2.0	EMERALD HEIGHTS	Fanshawe, J R	8	2	25.0	2	2		
96	0.5	EMILY'S LUCK CHARM (USA)	Stoute, Sir Michael	5	2	40.0	0	1		
91	6.0	EMMA PEEL	Meehan, B J	2	1	50.0	6			
99	1.0	EMPLANE (USA)	Cecil, H R A	4	1	25.0	1			
99	0.5	ENEMY ACTION (USA)	Cecil, H R A	4	2	50.0	1	0		
117	0.0	ENRIQUE	Cecil, H R A	3	2	66.7	0	0		
109	2.0	EQUITY PRINCESS	Johnstone, M	8	1	12.5	2			
91	2.0	ETIZAAZ (USA)	Dunlop, J L	2	1	50.0	2			
93	1.0	ETTERBY PARK (USA)	Johnstone, M	8	2	25.0	1	1		
99	3.0	EVENING PROMISE	McMahon, B A	6	2	33.3	0	6		
104	3.0	EVENING WORLD (FR)	Cole, P F I	5	2	40.0	5	1		
114	2.0	EXCLUSIVE	Stoute, Sir Michael	4	1	25.0	2			
103	2.0	EXEAT (USA)	Gosden, J H M	4	1	25.0	2			
113	1.0	FA-EQ (IRE)	Suroor, S bin	3	1	33.3	1			
94	3.0	FAIR FLIGHT	Dunlop, E A L	7	2	28.6	1	5		
95	0.5	FAIRY QUEEN (IRE)	Loder, D R	2	2	100.0	0	1		
122	1.5	FAITHFUL SON (USA)	Suroor, S bin	4	2	50.0	0	3		
93	3.0	FANTASTIC LIGHT (USA)	Stoute, Sir Michael	3	2	66.7	3	3		
90	1.0	FARAWAY LASS	Huntingdon, Lord	7	1	14.3	1			
91	1.0	FEARBY CROSS (IRE)	Bethell, J D	4	1	25.0	1			
91	3.0	FERNY HILL (IRE)	Muir, W R	5	1	20.0	3			
93	2.0	FFESTINIOG (IRE)	Cole, P F I	8	1	12.5	2			
96	4.0	FILFILAH	Walwyn, P T	8	2	25.0	3	5		
109	6.0	FIRE DOME (IRE)	Nicholls, D	9	2	22.2	6	6		
92	2.3	FIRST MUSICAL	Brittain, M	11	4	36.4	1	2	4	2
105	4.3	FIZZED	Johnstone, M	4	3	75.0	5	5	3	
99	0.8	FLANDERS (IRE)	Easterby, T D	7	4	57.1	1	0	1	1
97	2.0	FLAVIAN	Candy, H	2	1	50.0	2			
90	1.0	FLINT KNAPPER	Wragg, G	3	1	33.3	1			
103	4.0	FLORAZI	Dunlop, J L	4	2	50.0	4	4		
108	4.7	FOR YOUR EYES ONLY	Easterby, T D	8	3	37.5	5	4	5	
102	1.0	FRAGRANT OASIS (USA)	Dunlop, E A L	4	1	25.0	1			
100	6.0	FRIAR TUCK	Perratt, Miss L A	6	1	16.7	6			
115	4.0	FRUITS OF LOVE (USA)	Johnstone, M	7	1	14.3	4			
115	2.3	GAELIC STORM	Johnstone, M	12	4	33.3	2	1	5	1
119	1.0	GARUDA (IRE)	Dunlop, J L	4	1	25.0	1			
101	5.0	GENEROSITY	Cole, P F I	5	2	40.0	5	5		
104	2.3	GENEROUS LIBRA	Dunlop, J L	11	3	27.3	2	0	5	
103	2.0	GENEROUS ROSI	Dunlop, J L	8	1	12.5	2			
104	3.0	GENEROUS TERMS	Candy, H	3	2	66.7	6	0		
94	4.5	GEORGETTE (USA)	Gosden, J H M	3	2	66.7	6	3		
121	5.0	GERMANO	Wragg, G	4	1	25.0	5			
103	0.0	GHALIB (IRE)	Tregoning, M P	4	1	25.0	0			
91	2.0	GIPSY MOTH	Meehan, B J	7	1	14.3	2			
96	2.0	GIPSY ROSE LEE (IRE)	Meehan, B J	3	2	66.7	2	2		

71

Raceform rating	Average winning rating	Racehorse	Trainer	Number of runs	Number of wins	Winning %	Position in the betting, when winning			
100	0.0	GLAMIS (USA)	Gosden, J H M	5	1	20.0	0			
93	0.5	GOLDEN FORTUNE	Loder, D R	4	2	50.0	0	1		
99	2.0	GOLDEN SILCA	Channon, M R	8	4	50.0	2	1	2	3
111	2.0	GORSE	Candy, H	6	3	50.0	3	1	2	
100	4.0	GRANNY'S PET	Cole, P F I	7	1	14.3	4			
108	2.0	GRAZIA	Prescott, Sir Mark	2	1	50.0	2			
119	0.8	GREAT DANE (IRE)	Cecil, H R A	6	4	66.7	0	0	2	1
114	1.5	GREEK DANCE (IRE)	Stoute, Sir Michael	3	2	66.7	1	2		
109	2.0	GREEK PALACE (IRE)	Stoute, Sir Michael	4	1	25.0	2			
105	3.0	GREEN CARD (USA)	Woods, S P C	7	2	28.6	2	4		
92	1.5	GREY PRINCESS (IRE)	Harris, P W	7	4	57.1	3	1	1	1
98	0.0	GUINEA HUNTER (IRE)	Easterby, T D	3	1	33.3	0			
120	0.0	GULLAND	Wragg, G	3	1	33.3	0			
97	3.0	GYPSY PASSION (IRE)	Johnstone, M	5	1	20.0	3			
103	0.5	HAAFIZ (IRE)	Hanbury, B	4	2	50.0	1	0		
117	5.0	HAAMI (USA)	Dunlop, J L	5	1	20.0	5			
90	0.0	HABUB (USA)	Gosden, J H M	2	1	50.0	0			
93	1.5	HAJR (IRE)	Dunlop, E A L	6	2	33.3	1	2		
118	1.0	HANDSOME RIDGE	Gosden, J H M	4	1	25.0	1			
100	1.0	HASTY WORDS (IRE)	Hills, B W	6	1	16.7	1			
92	3.0	HAWADETH	Tregoning, M P	5	1	20.0	3			
97	2.0	HEAVENLY RAY (USA)	Fanshawe, J R	3	1	33.3	2			
91	3.0	HENRY HALL (IRE)	Tinkler, N	8	3	37.5	4	3	2	
93	1.0	HERB OF GRACE	Cecil, Mrs J	6	2	33.3	1	1		
114	2.0	HIGH AND LOW	Hills, B W	4	1	25.0	2			
126	3.0	HIGH-RISE (IRE)	Cumani, L M	5	3	60.0	1	2	6	
90	1.5	HIGH SPIRITS (IRE)	Easterby, T D	11	2	18.2	2	1		
94	2.0	HILL MAGIC	Elsworth, D R C	7	1	14.3	4			
95	3.0	HIMSELF (USA)	Cecil, H R A	5	2	40.0	5	1		
112	1.0	HITMAN (IRE)	Cecil, H R A	6	2	33.3	1	1		
105	5.5	HO LENG (IRE)	Perratt, Miss L A	6	2	33.3	6	5		
107	4.0	HORNBEAM	Jenkins, J R	7	1	14.3	4			
98	4.0	HOUSEKEEPER (IRE)	Charlton, R	3	1	33.3	4			
95	5.0	HOUSEMASTER (IRE)	Bell, M	5	1	20.0	5			
101	5.0	HOUSTON TIME (USA)	Loder, D R	2	1	50.0	5			
103	1.0	HUJOOM (IRE)	Dunlop, J L	6	1	16.7	1			
103	3.5	HULA ANGEL (USA)	Hills, B W	6	2	33.3	2	5		
95	4.5	HUNTERS OF BRORA (IRE)	Bethell, J D	9	2	22.2	6	3		
95	3.0	ICE	Johnstone, M	7	3	42.9	2	3	4	
91	0.0	IFTITAH (USA)	Suroor, S bin	1	1	100.0	0			
103	1.0	IMPERIAL BEAUTY (USA)	Makin, P J	3	1	33.3	1			
104	2.7	I'M PROPOSIN (IRE)	Dunlop, J L	3	3	100.0	3	0	5	
93	1.0	INCA TERN	Bravery, G C	7	2	28.6	1	1		
99	0.0	INDIANA LEGEND (IRE)	Meehan, B J	5	1	20.0	0			
93	4.0	INDIAN MISSILE	Chappell, Major D N	9	1	11.1	4			
91	5.0	INDIAN PLUME	Thornton, C W	3	1	33.3	5			
90	2.0	INDIMAAJ	Dunlop, J L	8	1	12.5	2			
109	1.0	INNUENDO (IRE)	Cumani, L M	5	3	60.0	1	1	1	

72

Raceform rating	Average winning rating	Racehorse	Trainer	Number of runs	Number of wins	Winning %	Position in the betting, when winning		
125	1.5	INSATIABLE (IRE)	Stoute, Sir Michael	6	2	33.3	1	2	
131	1.0	INTIKHAB (USA)	Suroor, S bin	2	2	100.0	1	1	
109	3.3	INVERMARK	Fanshawe, J R	7	3	42.9	0	4	6
97	2.8	INYA LAKE	Channon, M R	8	4	50.0	2 1 2 6		
93	0.0	ISCAN (IRE)	Stoute, Sir Michael	3	1	33.3	0		
90	1.0	ISHTIHAR (USA)	Suroor, S bin	2	1	50.0	1		
102	1.0	ISLAND SANDS (IRE)	Elsworth, D R C	2	2	100.0	2	0	
109	2.0	ISMAROS	Cecil, H R A	4	1	25.0	2		
93	1.0	IVORY CROWN (IRE)	Dunlop, E A L	9	1	11.1	1		
94	5.0	JAAZIM (USA)	Stoute, Sir Michael	6	1	16.7	5		
101	2.0	JALAAB (IRE)	Armstrong, R W	4	2	50.0	1	3	
103	3.5	JAZIL	Gosden, J H M	6	2	33.3	4	3	
91	1.0	JENNELLE	Dwyer, C A	7	1	14.3	1		
106	0.0	JIBE (USA)	Cecil, H R A	4	1	25.0	0		
101	1.0	JILA (IRE)	Armstrong, R W	3	2	66.7	1	1	
97	1.0	JINSIYAH (USA)	Hanbury, B	5	1	20.0	1		
106	5.0	JO MELL	Easterby, T D	8	1	12.5	5		
106	4.0	JOSR ALGARHOUD (IRE)	Channon, M R	2	1	50.0	4		
108	0.0	KADAKA (IRE)	Cumani, L M	5	1	20.0	0		
103	3.0	KAHTAN	Dunlop, J L	4	1	25.0	3		
93	0.0	KALIDASA (USA)	Chapple-Hyam, P W	6	1	16.7	0		
92	1.3	KARASI (IRE)	Stoute, Sir Michael	9	3	33.3	0	3	1
92	1.0	KAREYMAH	Loder, D R	2	2	100.0	0	2	
93	0.0	KARIYH (USA)	Dunlop, J L	6	1	16.7	0		
123	3.0	KAYF TARA	Suroor, S bin	5	3	60.0	1	5	3
92	1.5	KAYO	Etherington, T J	10	2	20.0	1	2	
92	2.5	KELD (IRE)	Fanshawe, J R	3	2	66.7	4	1	
93	6.0	KEWARRA	Millman, B R	9	1	11.1	6		
94	1.0	KHEYRAH (USA)	Dunlop, E A L	2	1	50.0	1		
104	0.0	KING ADAM (IRE)	Stoute, Sir Michael	3	1	33.3	0		
123	2.0	KING OF KINGS (IRE)	O'Brien, A P	2	1	50.0	2		
102	4.0	KING SLAYER	Smart, B	9	1	11.1	4		
107	2.0	KISMAH	Stewart, A C	2	2	100.0	2	2	
117	1.7	KISSOGRAM	Cumani, L M	4	3	75.0	4	0	1
98	3.0	KRISPY KNIGHT	Hills, J W	1	1	100.0	3		
93	0.0	KRISTINA	Stoute, Sir Michael	2	1	50.0	0		
105	2.0	KUMAIT (USA)	Dunlop, E A L	9	1	11.1	2		
103	0.0	KUMATOUR	Cumani, L M	5	1	20.0	0		
105	1.0	LABEQ (IRE)	Walwyn, P T	9	1	11.1	1		
90	3.0	LADY ANGHARAD	Jarvis, A P	7	2	28.6	5	1	
109	1.5	LADY IN WAITING	Cole, P F I	7	2	28.6	2	1	
90	1.0	LAGO DI VARANO	Whitaker, R M	19	1	5.3	1		
114	2.0	LAND OF DREAMS	Johnstone, M	6	1	16.7	2		
107	4.0	LARGESSE	Berry, John	9	3	33.3	5	2	5
94	5.0	LATE NIGHT OUT	Jarvis, W	4	1	25.0	5		
105	0.0	LAURENTIDE (USA)	Cecil, H R A	3	1	33.3	0		

Raceform rating	Average winning rating	Racehorse	Trainer	Number of runs	Number of wins	Winning %	Position in the betting, when winning		
108	3.5	LEAR SPEAR (USA)	Elsworth, D R C	10	2	20.0	1	6	
90	1.0	LIGHTNING ARROW (USA)	Dunlop, J L	4	1	25.0	1		
90	2.5	LIGHT THE ROCKET	Hannon, R	6	2	33.3	3	2	
107	4.0	LILLI CLAIRE	Elsworth, D R C	11	2	18.2	6	2	
94	2.7	LITERARY SOCIETY (USA)	Toller, J A R	6	3	50.0	1	1	6
115	2.0	LOCHANGEL	Balding, I A	8	2	25.0	1	3	
103	3.5	LOCOMBE HILL (IRE)	Blanshard, M	5	2	40.0	6	1	
96	1.0	LONELY HEART	Elsworth, D R C	3	1	33.3	1		
101	5.5	LONE PIPER	Brittain, C E	7	2	28.6	5	6	
98	0.5	LONESOME DUDE	Stoute, Sir Michael	6	2	33.3	0	1	
112	0.0	LORD OF MEN	Gosden, J H M	4	1	25.0	0		
93	2.0	LOUGH SWILLY (IRE)	Hills, B W	5	2	40.0	1	3	
118	1.5	LOVERS KNOT	Stoute, Sir Michael	6	2	33.3	2	1	
111	0.0	LUCAYAN INDIAN (IRE)	Loder, D R	3	1	33.3	0		
120	0.0	LUJAIN (USA)	Loder, D R	4	3	75.0	0	0	0
94	1.0	MAGHAARB	Tregoning, M P	2	1	50.0	1		
96	2.0	MAGNO (USA)	Cole, P F I	4	1	25.0	2		
104	5.0	MAIDAAN	Channon, M R	2	1	50.0	5		
110	4.0	MARCH STAR (IRE)	Toller, J A R	7	2	28.6	3	5	
105	2.0	MARCUS MAXIMUS (USA)	Cecil, H R A	3	2	66.7	0	4	
116	1.5	MARIDPOUR (IRE)	Stoute, Sir Michael	6	2	33.3	0	3	
91	1.0	MARTON MOSS (SWE)	Easterby, T D	15	1	6.7	1		
95	3.0	MASHA-II (IRE)	Gosden, J H M	9	2	22.2	5	1	
99	1.5	MAWARED (IRE)	Dunlop, J L	3	2	66.7	1	2	
95	1.5	MAWSOOF	Stoute, Sir Michael	5	2	40.0	0	3	
110	5.0	MIDNIGHT ESCAPE	Wall, C F	6	1	16.7	5		
113	1.0	MIDNIGHT LINE (USA)	Cecil, H R A	4	1	25.0	1		
95	1.0	MIHNAH (IRE)	Tregoning, M P	3	1	33.3	1		
91	1.0	MINNESOTA	Callaghan, N A	8	1	12.5	1		
98	1.0	MISBAH (USA)	Hanbury, B	5	1	20.0	1		
90	2.0	MISS AMANPURI	Wragg, G	4	1	25.0	2		
99	1.0	MISS UNIVERSE (IRTE)	Hills, B W	7	1	14.3	1		
93	1.0	MITCHAM (IRE)	Mills, T G	3	1	33.3	1		
94	1.5	MIZHAR (USA)	Dunlop, E A L	4	2	50.0	2	1	
112	1.0	MONAASSIB	Dunlop, E A L	7	1	14.3	1		
90	2.0	MONDSCHEIN	Dunlop, J L	5	1	20.0	2		
91	0.0	MONITOR	Cecil, H R A	7	1	14.3	0		
99	1.7	MONKSTON POINT (IRE)	Arbuthnot, D W P	8	3	37.5	3	0	2
92	0.0	MORATORIUM (USA)	Cecil, H R A	5	1	20.0	0		
98	0.0	MOTHER OF PEARL (IRE)	Chapple-Hyam, P W	1	1	100.0	0		
111	1.0	MOUNTAIN SONG	Prescott, Sir Mark	5	2	40.0	2	0	
106	0.0	MOWBRAY (USA)	Cole, P F I	5	1	20.0	0		
99	1.3	MOWELGA	Herries, Lady	6	3	50.0	2	1	1
92	1.0	MR CAHILL (USA)	Stoute, Sir Michael	5	1	20.0	1		
103	0.5	MUBRIK (IRE)	Gosden, J H M	5	2	40.0	0	1	
116	4.0	MUCHEA	Channon, M R	8	2	25.0	2	6	
103	2.0	MUHIB (USA)	Stoute, Sir Michael	5	2	40.0	0	4	
92	3.0	MUHTAFEL	Jenkins, J R	13	2	15.4	2	4	

Raceform rating	Average winning rating	Racehorse	Trainer	Number of runs	Number of wins	Winning %	Position in the betting, when winning					
121	0.7	MUHTATHIR	Gosden, J H M	7	3	42.9	0	1	1			
116	2.7	MUJAHID (USA)	Dunlop, J L	4	3	75.0	2	0	6			
102	1.5	MUKHALIF (IRE)	Loder, D R	2	2	100.0	2	1				
117	5.0	MULTICOLOURED (IRE)	Stoute, Sir Michael	4	1	25.0	5					
100	3.5	MUQTARIB (USA)	Dunlop, J L	3	2	66.7	3	4				
100	2.0	MURGHEM (IRE)	Hanbury, B	9	1	11.1	2					
98	1.0	MUSHRAAF	Dunlop, J L	3	1	33.3	1					
98	2.0	MUTAAHAB (CAN)	Dunlop, E A L	6	4	66.7	2	0	3	3		
92	1.0	MUTAFAWEQ (USA)	Suroor, S bin	2	1	50.0	1					
120	0.7	MUTAMAM	Stewart, A C	6	3	50.0	1	0	1			
110	0.0	MUTAWWAJ (IRE)	Suroor, S bin	4	1	25.0	0					
100	1.0	MYTHICAL GIRL (USA)	Loder, D R	3	2	66.7	1	1				
111	3.5	NANOUSHKA (IRE)	Hannon, R	6	2	33.3	2	5				
100	6.0	NAPOLEON'S SISTER (IRE)	Elsworth, D R C	6	1	16.7	6					
91	0.5	NASHEED (USA)	Dunlop, J L	3	2	66.7	0	1				
94	2.7	NASKHI	Johnston, M	13	3	23.1	4	4	0			
94	5.0	NAUTICAL STAR	Hills, J W	6	2	33.3	5	5				
117	2.0	NEDAWI	Suroor, S bin	4	3	75.0	2	3	1			
110	1.3	NIGHT SHOT	Balding, I A	12	3	25.0	1	2	1			
107	3.0	NIGRASINE	Eyre, J L	13	1	7.7	3					
92	1.0	NOBLE ONE	Prescott, Sir Mark	1	1	100.0	1					
94	2.0	NO EXTRAS (IRE)	Moore, G L	12	1	8.3	2					
98	1.5	NUCLEAR DEBATE (USA)	Ramsden, Mrs J R	9	2	22.2	1	2				
101	1.8	ON CALL	Prescott, Sir Mark	9	6	66.7	4	0	0	0	3	4
118	2.5	ONE SO WONDERFUL	Cumani, L M	5	2	40.0	1	4				
98	0.0	ON THE RIDGE (IRE)	Cecil, H R A	4	1	25.0	0					
98	2.0	OPERA KING (USA)	Suroor, S bin	2	1	50.0	2					
92	0.0	ORIENTAL FASHION (IRE)	Suroor, S bin	2	1	50.0	0					
93	3.0	ORMELIE (IRE)	Chapple-Hyam, P W	5	2	40.0	3	3				
90	1.7	PAIRUMANI STAR (IRE)	Dunlop, J L	9	3	33.3	2	1	2			
100	2.0	PANTAR (IRE)	Balding, I A	9	1	11.1	2					
98	3.0	PARISIEN STAR (IRE)	Lewis, G	8	2	25.0	2	4				
98	0.0	PATRIOT	Smart, B	7	1	14.3	0					
112	2.0	PEAK PATH (IRE)	Stoute, Sir Michael	3	1	33.3	2					
92	5.0	PEARTREE HOUSE (IRE)	Muir, W R	5	1	20.0	5					
90	2.0	PECULIARITY	Smart, B	3	1	33.3	2					
105	0.0	PEGNITZ (USA)	Brittain, C E	6	1	16.7	0					
102	5.0	PERFECT PARADIGM (IRE)	Gosden, J H M	9	1	11.1	5					
92	2.0	PERRYSTON VIEW	Calver, P	6	1	16.7	2					
99	1.7	PERSIANO	Fanshawe, J R	4	3	75.0	3	1	1			
120	1.7	PERSIAN PUNCH (IRE)	Elsworth, D R C	5	3	60.0	2	1	2			
103	2.5	PERUGINO BAY (IRE)	McMahon, B A	10	2	20.0	1	4				
98	1.0	PERUSING (IRE)	Cumani, L M	5	2	40.0	0	2				
92	1.0	PET EXPRESS FLYER (IRE)	Haslam, P C	10	3	30.0	1	0	2			
100	1.3	PIPALONG (IRE)	Easterby, T D	6	3	50.0	2	1	1			
104	0.5	PISTACHIO	Fanshawe, J R	6	2	33.3	1	0				
99	2.0	PLAN-B	Gosden, J H M	4	1	25.0	2					

Raceform rating	Average winning rating	Racehorse	Trainer	Number of runs	Number of wins	Winning %	Position in the betting, when winning		
98	1.0	POLES APART (IRE)	Tompkins, M H	4	1	25.0	1		
102	2.0	PORTO FORICOS (USA)	Cecil, H R A	8	2	25.0	0	4	
106	4.0	POSEIDON	Channon, M R	6	1	16.7	4		
122	3.0	POSIDONAS	Cole, P F I	5	2	40.0	3	3	
91	3.3	PREMIER GENERATION (IRE)	Arbuthnot, D W P	14	3	21.4	2	4	4
93	2.5	PREMIER NIGHT	Dow, S	5	2	40.0	2	3	
103	3.0	PRESENT ARMS (USA)	Cole, P F I	8	1	12.5	3		
94	5.0	PRIMO LARA	Harris, P W	5	1	20.0	5		
101	1.0	PRINCE BABAR	Banks, J E	7	1	14.3	1		
98	4.0	PRINCE OF DENIAL	Arbuthnot, D W P	8	1	12.5	4		
92	0.0	PRINCIPALITY (IRE)	Berry, J	10	1	10.0	0		
112	1.5	PROLIX	Hills, B W	7	2	28.6	1	2	
112	4.7	PROUD NATIVE (IRE)	Nicholls, D	12	3	25.0	6	5	3
98	4.0	PUNISHMENT	Cunningham-Brown, K O	9	1	11.1	4		
96	1.5	PUTUNA	Balding, I A	9	2	22.2	2	1	
103	1.0	QHAZEEENAH	Dunlop, J L	5	2	40.0	1	1	
97	4.0	QILIN (IRE)	Tompkins, M H	10	1	10.0	4		
94	1.0	QUEENSLAND STAR (IRE)	Berry, J	10	2	20.0	1	1	
114	3.0	RABAH	Dunlop, J L	6	3	50.0	4	3	2
93	3.0	RACHAELS NORTH (IRE)	Armstrong, R W	8	2	25.0	2	4	
93	1.0	RAFFAELLO (IRE)	Channon, M R	6	1	16.7	1		
109	3.5	RAINALD (USA)	Gosden, J H M	4	2	50.0	4	3	
96	3.0	RAINBOW HIGH	Hills, B W	6	1	16.7	3		
93	3.0	RAINBOW WAYS	Hills, B W	6	3	50.0	0	5	4
106	1.3	RAISE A GRAND (IRE)	Payne, J W	6	3	50.0	1	1	2
92	4.3	RAISE A PRINCE (FRA)	Woods, S P C	10	3	30.0	5	5	3
98	5.0	RAJAIYMA (IRE)	Cumani, L M	3	1	33.3	5		
94	1.5	RAKEEB (USA)	Stewart, A C	6	2	33.3	1	2	
109	2.0	RAMBLING BEAR	Blanshard, M	10	1	10.0	2		
110	3.0	RAMBLING ROSE	Stoute, Sir Michael	4	1	25.0	3		
109	1.0	RAMOOZ (USA)	Hanbury, B	11	2	18.2	1	1	
115	1.5	REDBRIDGE (USA)	Gosden, J H M	6	2	33.3	1	2	
93	1.0	RED DELIRIUM	Hannon, R	11	1	9.1	1		
90	3.5	RED LION	Payne, J W	5	2	40.0	5	2	
102	2.7	RED PRAIRIE (USA)	Bell, M	7	3	42.9	2	2	4
91	1.0	RED RAMONA	Akehurst, J	7	1	14.3	1		
105	4.0	RED SEA	Cole, P F I	5	2	40.0	2	2	
95	6.0	REFUSE TO LOSE	Eustace, J M P	6	1	16.7	6		
108	4.0	REPERTORY	Saunders, M S	9	2	22.2	3	5	
99	3.0	RETURN OF AMIN	Bethell, J D	10	1	10.0	3		
95	3.0	RHAPSODIST (USA)	Gosden, J H M	4	1	25.0	3		
92	3.5	RICH IN LOVE	Cyzer, C A	14	2	14.3	6	1	
100	3.0	RIGHT WING (IRE)	Dunlop, J L	7	1	14.3	3		
100	4.0	RISQUE LADY	Harris, P W	9	1	11.1	4		
91	1.5	RIVERBLUE (IRE)	Ramsden, Mrs J R	6	2	33.3	0	3	
102	4.0	ROCK FALCON	Herries, Lady	9	3	33.3	5	5	2
105	2.5	ROKEBY BOWL	Balding, I A	8	2	25.0	2	3	
117	3.0	ROMANOV (IRE)	Chapple-Hyam, P W	3	1	33.3	3		

Raceform rating	Average winning rating	Racehorse	Trainer	Number of runs	Number of wins	Winning %	Position in the betting, when winning		
98	4.0	ROSE OF MOONCOIN	Banks, J E	3	1	33.3	4		
102	3.0	ROSSELLI (USA)	Berry, J	5	3	60.0	1	3	5
125	1.3	ROYAL ANTHEM (USA)	Cecil, H R A	5	3	60.0	3	0	1
115	5.0	RUSSIAN REVIVAL (USA)	Gosden, J H M	5	1	20.0	5		
95	4.0	RUSTIC (IRE)	Charlton, R	3	1	33.3	4		
90	3.7	SAAFEND ROCK	Hannon, R	8	3	37.5	5	1	5
114	2.5	SAAFEYA (IRE)	Gosden, J H M	4	2	50.0	2	3	
111	2.0	SABADILLA	Gosden, J H M	4	1	25.0	2		
115	1.3	SADIAN	Dunlop, J L	7	3	42.9	1	3	0
102	1.0	SAILING SHOES (IRE)	Hannon, R	6	1	16.7	1		
102	1.5	SAKHA	Dunlop, J L	3	2	66.7	1	2	
96	0.0	SALMON LADDER (USA)	Cole, P F I	9	2	22.2	0	0	
93	1.0	SAMUT (IRE)	Gosden, J H M	3	1	33.3	1		
112	2.0	SANTILLANA (USA)	Gosden, J H M	3	1	33.3	2		
95	1.0	SARSON	Hannon, R	5	1	20.0	1		
90	1.0	SAYTARRA (USA)	Loder, D R	1	1	100.0	1		
93	1.0	SCATTERGUN	Gosden, J H M	5	1	20.0	1		
116	2.0	SCORNED (GER)	Balding, I A	7	3	42.9	1	1	4
122	1.3	SEA WAVE (IRE)	Suroor, S bin	5	3	60.0	0	1	3
105	4.5	SECRET ARCHIVE	Hannon, R	7	2	28.6	4	5	
103	2.0	SECRET SAVER (USA)	Stoute, Sir Michael	4	2	50.0	2	2	
101	4.0	SEIGNORIAL (USA)	Chapple-Hyam, P W	5	2	40.0	2	6	
105	5.5	SELHURSTPARK FLYER (IRE)	Berry, J	8	2	25.0	5	6	
106	4.0	SENSORY	Hills, B W	7	1	14.3	4		
95	5.0	SERGEANT YORK	Smith, C	7	1	14.3	5		
92	2.0	SERPENTINE	Fanshawe, J R	3	1	33.3	2		
92	2.0	SHALAD'OR	Millman, B R	8	2	25.0	2	2	
109	1.5	SHARP PLAY	Johnston, M	4	2	50.0	0	3	
110	5.0	SHEER DANZIG	Armstrong, R W	4	1	25.0	5		
105	5.0	SHEER VIKING (IRE)	Hills, B W	7	2	28.6	5	5	
100	2.0	SHELTERING SKY (IRE)	Dunlop, J L	6	1	16.7	2		
104	3.0	SHFOUG (USA)	Hills, B W	10	3	30.0	3	3	3
91	0.0	SHIMAAL	Suroor, S bin	3	1	33.3	0		
104	0.0	SICNEE (USA)	Loder, D R	3	1	33.3	0		
99	4.0	SIGNORINA CATTIVA (USA)	Dunlop, J L	2	1	50.0	4		
108	3.0	SILENCE REIGNS	Stoute, Sir Michael	7	1	14.3	3		
93	2.8	SILK ST JOHN	Ryan, M J	15	4	26.7	0	4	3	4
122	2.0	SILVER PATRIARCH (IRE)	Dunlop, J L	6	1	16.7	2		
110	2.0	SILVER RHAPSODY (USA)	Cecil, H R A	4	2	50.0	2	2	
105	4.0	SMITTENBY (IRE)	Duffield, Mrs P N	9	2	22.2	2	6	
95	2.0	SOCIETY SNOOP (IRE)	Johnston, M	5	1	20.0	2		
90	2.5	SOMAYDA (IRE)	Dunlop, J L	4	2	50.0	1	4	
100	1.0	SONG OF FREEDOM	Gosden, J H M	6	1	16.7	1		
100	0.5	SOUFFLE	Cecil, H R A	6	2	33.3	0	1	
112	3.5	SOVIET BUREAU (IRE)	Kelleway, Miss Gay	7	2	28.6	5	2	
92	0.5	SPANISH FERN (USA)	Charlton, R	4	2	50.0	0	1	
107	1.0	SPEEDFIT TOO (IRE)	Margarson, G G	6	1	16.7	1		

Raceform rating	Average winning rating	Racehorse	Trainer	Number of runs	Number of wins	Winning %	Position in the betting, when winning			
97	0.5	SPEEDY JAMES (IRE)	Berry, J	7	2	28.6	1	0		
102	1.5	SPINDRIFT (IRE)	Cumani, L M	2	2	100.0	1	2		
112	3.5	SPIRIT OF LOVE (USA)	Johnston, M	6	4	66.7	3	1	5	5
97	1.0	SPIRIT WILLING (IRE)	Loder, D R	4	1	25.0	1			
92	4.0	SPUNKIE	Johnson-Houghton, R F	5	2	40.0	6	2		
98	1.5	STAR CRYSTAL (IRE)	Cecil, H R A	5	2	40.0	3	0		
99	1.0	SUBEEN	Loder, D R	3	1	33.3	1			
94	2.0	SUBITO	Cumani, L M	4	1	25.0	2			
101	1.0	SUCCESS AND GLORY (IRE)	Cecil, H R A	3	1	33.3	1			
104	2.7	SUGARFOOT	Tinkler, N	10	3	30.0	5	2	1	
94	3.5	SUNLEY SENSE	Channon, M R	11	2	18.2	5	2		
102	2.3	SUNSTREAK	Wall, C F	6	3	50.0	3	2	2	
107	2.7	SUPERIOR PREMIUM	Fahey, R A	10	3	30.0	1	2	5	
99	1.0	SUPPLY AND DEMAND	Moore, G L	7	1	14.3	1			
100	3.6	SUPREME SOUND	Harris, P W	14	5	35.7	3	5	2	3 5
101	4.0	SWEETNESS HERSELF	Ryan, M J	9	2	22.2	4	4		
105	1.0	TADEO	Johnston, M	9	2	22.2	1	1		
100	1.0	TADWIGA	Hannon, R	6	3	50.0	1	0	2	
97	2.0	TAYIL (IRE)	Dunlop, J L	5	2	40.0	2	2		
111	4.0	TEDBURROW	Alston, E J	9	3	33.3	5	5	2	
93	0.5	TEMERAIRE (USA)	Perrett, Mrs A J	5	2	40.0	0	1		
93	1.0	THICKET	Charlton, R	3	1	33.3	1			
93	4.0	TIMAHS	Loder, D R	2	1	50.0	4			
114	3.3	TIPSY CREEK (USA)	Hanbury, B	8	3	37.5	2	3	5	
109	3.0	TRACKING	Cecil, H R A	4	1	25.0	3			
93	2.7	TRAVELMATE	Fanshawe, J R	6	3	50.0	3	3	2	
107	0.5	TUNING	Cecil, H R A	5	2	40.0	0	1		
97	3.3	TWO CLUBS	Cecil, Mrs J	4	3	75.0	3	5	2	
99	3.5	UNDETERRED	Wall, C F	4	2	50.0	2	5		
100	2.0	VALENTINE GIRL	Hills, B W	3	1	33.3	2			
100	2.0	VALENTINE WALTZ (IRE)	Gosden, J H M	4	1	25.0	2			
102	1.0	VISION OF NIGHT	Dunlop, J L	4	2	50.0	1	1		
101	2.5	VOLONTIERS	Harris, P W	9	2	22.2	1	4		
103	1.0	WAHJ	Stoute, Sir Michael	2	2	100.0	0	2		
104	2.3	WANNABE GRAND (IRE)	Noseda, J	8	3	37.5	1	5	1	
104	1.0	WARNINGFORD	Fanshawe, J R	13	2	15.4	1	1		
92	2.0	WEALTHY STAR (IRE)	Hanbury, B	2	1	50.0	2			
97	2.3	WHITE HEART	Johnston, M	5	3	60.0	2	1	4	
98	0.0	WINCE	Cecil, H R A	6	2	33.3	0	0		
95	2.3	WUXI VENTURE	Woods, S P C	13	3	23.1	1	5	1	
114	3.0	YAVANA'S PACE (IRE)	Johnston, M	11	4	36.4	1	6	3	2
116	5.0	YORKIES BOY	McMahon, B A	7	2	28.6	5	5		
99	4.0	YULARA	Meehan, B J	6	2	33.3	5	3		
97	0.0	ZAAJER	Dunlop, E A L	2	1	50.0	0			
110	1.3	ZELANDA (IRE)	Gosden, J H M	6	3	50.0	2	0	2	
113	0.0	ZOMARADAH	Cumani, L M	3	1	33.3	0			

Chapter 5
Summary

In all, over three seasons, a total of 2,267 races were analyzed with a view to assessing how the betting market worked. The conclusions from this research and resultant recommendations can be summarised into three sections, the integrity of racing, administration and betting.

5.1 The integrity of racing

In the long term, it can be shown that the actual results are consistent with that predicted by the market. If racing's integrity were being compromised to any great extent, then such a finding would be impossible. Accordingly, the conclusion has to be that, to a greater extent, racing is being run fairly and although it would not be wise to become complacent, there are no grounds for major concerns.

There is evidence of insider trading in just under twenty per cent of all races. Mostly, exposed horses are being backed and the market response is that the betting margins are widened. The confirmation of this is the slight bias experienced where betting margins are greater than 2.5% per runner, compared with the mean of 2.0% per runner. In such cases, the first or second favourite wins sixty per cent of all races, compared with fifty per cent in the remainder of races (see Table 3-2) and one of the first four in the betting wins eighty per cent of high margin races, compared with just over seventy per cent in races where the margin is no higher than 2.5% per runner.

Unexposed horses, not in the first four in the betting, are subject to insider trading in about one and a half per cent of all races. The evidence for this is that the Tote odds, not being subject to insider trading as such activity would be self-defeating, are much higher than the outer limit of expectation, having taken into account the expected differences due to bookmakers harmonizing their odds as a defence against potential insider attack.

In most cases, insiders are backing (at the time) unexposed horses and the advantage they have is knowing the improvement their horses have made. There is no evidence that the rules of racing have been breached and one would only become concerned about the integrity of racing when such insider trading concerned horses who had not improved on previous runs.

5.2 Administration

It would be impossible to assess how the betting market worked if there was nothing to compare it to and there can be no doubt that it is advantageous to all to have competition through the dual system of bookmakers and Tote pools. It is very important that the administration of the industry and the betting market are independent of each other. It would not matter, for example, if the Tote were to be floated off as a public company, as long as the British Horseracing Board did not have a controlling interest. If they did, there may be the temptation to increase the percentage deductions from the Tote pools, in an effort to increase prize money. If such action were taken, then in the short term, off-course bookmakers' profitability would increase as odds were adjusted to reflect the competition, but in the long term betting turnover would decline.

A strategy that might have the desired effect of increasing prize money would be to ensure that an independent Tote was encouraged to increase its market share and motivated to continue its policy of helping the racing industry as much as possible. The way to do this would be to breach the illusion masterminded by the bookmakers that they offer better odds than the Tote. Bookmakers create this illusion by harmonizing the odds, so that the returns at starting prices will usually beat Tote returns if the first, second or third favourite wins and as such horses win more than sixty per cent of all races, they can demonstrate they beat the Tote, more often than not. What bookmakers do not advertise is the fact that whereas they beat the Tote by relatively small amounts when the harmonization is against them, the Tote returns are notably better than starting prices when the opposite applies.

However, when bookmakers are betting to high margins, to protect themselves against insider trading on one of the favourites, they are only just holding the line against the Tote. A strategy the Tote could adopt, therefore, would be to reduce their deduction from the win and place pool to 12% (from 16% and 24% respectively). The effect this would have would be to ensure Tote odds were greater than starting prices on all high betting margin races, irrespective of the result, and to ensure Tote dividends were closer to starting prices, where the first or second favourite won in a relatively low betting margin race. Overall, this action would help the Tote to increase market share.

5.3 Betting

Punters can use the betting market as a guide to help in their quest of profitable betting, by taking the following steps:

1) Assess the market for signs of insider trading relative to unexposed horses.

2) If no evidence of such insider trading, roughly calculate the betting margin on the race. If this exceeds 2.5% per runner, do not bet.

3) Assuming the betting margin on the race is not greater than 2.5% per runner, review selection if it is not in the first four in the betting (won by more than 70% of all races). Use other 'checking tables' found in this book.

4) Having reviewed and finalised selection, use chart (Table 3-9) to evaluate whether to back with bookmakers, or at starting prices, or at Tote odds, if all the information needed to make this decision is not available to you.